SAT® Vocabulary
A New Approach

Second Edition

Larry Krieger and Erica L. Meltzer

◤THE CRITICAL READER

New York

ISBN- 13: 979-8-9873835-6-8

ALSO BY LARRY KRIEGER

. . . .

Crash Course - AP® US History

Crash Course - AP® European History

AP® Art History: Beyond the European Tradition with Global Contemporary

AP® US History, A Strategic Review

AP® US History: Doing the DBQ

AP® US History: Fast Review

AP® US History: Mastering Multiple Choice

War and Destiny: Russia and Ukraine

ALSO BY ERICA MELTZER

. . . .

The Ultimate Guide to SAT® Grammar Workbook

The Critical Reader: The Complete Guide to SAT® Reading

The Critical Reader: AP® English Language and Composition Edition

The Complete Guide to ACT® English

The Complete Guide to ACT® Reading

The Complete GMAT® Sentence Correction Guide

GRE® Vocabulary in Practice

How to Write for Class: A Student's Guide to Grammar, Punctuation, and Style

IELTS® Writing: Grammar and Vocabulary

Table of Contents

	Part 1: Core Words	7
	Introduction: Vocabulary Is Important!	9
1.	The DSAT® and 10 Tough Words	17
2.	The DSAT and an American Icon	20
3.	The DSAT, J. Robert Oppenheimer, and the Atomic Bomb	23
4.	The DSAT Goes to the Movies	26
5.	The DSAT, Taylor Swift, and the Eras Tour	29
6.	The DSAT and the Demise of the Dinosaurs	32
7.	The DSAT and the DART Mission	35
8.	The DSAT and Words with a History	38
9.	The DSAT and American History	41
10.	The DSAT and the Mighty Prefix	45
11.	The DSAT and the Mighty Suffix	49
	Part 2: Vocabulary in Context	53
12.	Sentence Completions: Basic Strategies	55
13.	Sentence Completions: Advanced Strategies	64
	Matching Key Words and Phrases: Synonyms and Antonyms	71
	Independent Practice: Sentence Completions	81
14.	Meaning in Context: Multi-Meaning Words	98
	Part 3: Transitional Words and Phrases	107
15.	Types of Transitions	109
16.	Continuation	116
17.	Sequence	123
18.	Reversal	128
19.	Cause and Effect	135
	Independent Practice: All Transitions	141

Part 1:
Core Words

Introduction: Vocabulary Is Important!

Let's begin with the good news: the new Digital SAT is shorter than the old paper and pencil SAT. But is it easier? "I went in so confident," reported a Reddit poster. However, the student's confidence did not last for long. "Five minutes later I was panicking over *evince* and *preclude*." Other concerned students underscored this widespread feeling of concern by reporting that they did not know the meaning of challenging DSAT words such as *engender*, *ineluctable*, and *innocuous*.

Although the DSAT will not directly ask you to define vocabulary words, each Reading and Writing module will begin with a series of sentence-completion questions that ask you to complete a sentence "with the most logical and precise word or phrase." In addition, another series of questions later in the module will ask you to complete a text "with the most logical transition." Taken together, the sentence completion and transition questions make up about thirty percent of the 54 questions on your two DSAT Reading and Writing modules.

Thirty percent is a lot! It means that a strong vocabulary is crucial to earning a high DSAT score. But the English language contains just over 1 million words, the most of any modern language. If each of these words had an equal chance of appearing on the DSAT, studying for vocabulary questions would be an impossible task.

But fear not! The lexicon, or pool, of possible vocabulary words, is not unlimited or impossible to find. In order to create a scoring system that is valid and replicable, the test writers must draw upon a carefully selected and tested group of words. These words are actually hiding in plain sight, right in the tests themselves.

Taking advantage of the College Board's strict testing standards, we have compiled a list of 250 vocabulary words that you must absolutely, positively know. **We created our list by beginning with both correct and incorrect answers on released DSATs, as reported by a large group of students who have already sat for the test.** It is important to keep in mind that "incorrect" and "correct" answers are not fixed categories: a wrong **answer in one module can and may be the right answer in a different module.** For this reason, the practice questions in this book sometimes feature the same words as both correct and incorrect answers.

Part 1 begins with our list of 250 vocabulary words that have appeared on DSAT modules. We were not content to compile the best list of DSAT vocabulary words—we also want to help you remember them. Chapters 1-11 use vivid examples drawn from a variety of popular topics, including recent movies such as *Barbie*, *Oppenheimer*, and *Avengers: Endgame* to illustrate 110 of the very top words. We are confident that these chapters will help you increase your vocabulary and raise your DSAT score!

Then, in Parts 2 and 3, things get more a bit more serious. You'll be asked to apply your knowledge to test-style questions that reflect the content and level of the real exam (unfortunately, the DSAT is unlikely to include passages about *Barbie*!). Ready? Let's go.

20 KEY WORDS: THE ALL-IMPORTANT "CLAIM" CLUSTER

You MUST learn these 20 words! Really, we're not kidding or exaggerating. The CLAIM cluster includes the most frequently used words on Reading and Writing modules. Why is this true? A CLAIM is an assertion. The authors selected by College Board test writers often make a claim or assertion. This claim will then be supported with evidence and critically evaluated. We promise that achieving a full command of this all-important cluster of words will help you answer a number of DSAT question!

MAKING A CLAIM

1.   ADVANCE – to put forward a claim
2.   ASSERT – to put forward an argument or state that something is true
3.   CONJECTURE – n., hypothesis; v., hypothesize
4.   (PRE)SUPPOSITION – an idea assumed beforehand about a subject
5.   SURMISE – to assume; draw a conclusion without strong evidence

SUPPORTING A CLAIM

6.   BOLSTER – to provide support for an argument
7.   BUTTRESS – to provide support for an argument
8.   SUBSTANTIATE – to provide evidence to support or prove a claim
9.   CORROBORATE – to confirm or support a claim
10. VALIDATE – to prove the accuracy of a claim

RECOGNIZING A CLAIM

11. CONCEDE – to admit that an opposing claim is true or valid
12. ACKNOWLEDGE – to accept or admit the validity of a claim

QUESTIONING A CLAIM

13. REBUT – to offer an argument a against a claim believed to be false
14. REFUTE – to prove that a claim is false

THINKING ABOUT A CLAIM

15. GRAPPLE WITH – to try to deal with or understand a difficult problem
16. RUMINATE ABOUT – to think deeply about; turn something over in one's mind
17. INFER – to deduce or conclude from evidence and reasoning

SUPPORTING, CRITICIZING, AND DOUBTING A CLAIM

18. PROPONENT – person who supports a claim or course of action
19. DETRACTOR – person who criticizes a claim or course of action
20. SKEPTIC – person who questions or doubts a claim

CORE VOCABULARY

The words on this list are not randomly selected; they are CORE words because each has already appeared as a right or wrong answer on a DSAT. It is important to note that students are already reporting that words encountered on one test are reappearing on another test.

21. ABRUPT – sudden or unexpected
22. ADAMANT – extremely stubborn; fixed in one's viewpoint
23. ABUNDANT – plentiful
24. ACCENTUATE – to make more noticeable or prominent
25. ACCLAIM – enthusiastic and public praise
26. ADAPTATION – a change made to accommodate new circumstances
27. ADVANTAGEOUS – creating favorable circumstances
28. AESTHETIC – related to the study or appreciation of beauty
29. AFFECTING – touching the emotions; moving
30. AFFINITY - a strong attraction or liking
31. AMBIGUOUS – unclear; open to more than one interpretation
32. AMBIVALENCE – having mixed feelings
33. AMELIORATE – to make better; improve
34. AMORPHOUS – shapeless; synonym for "nebulous"
35. ANALOGY – a comparison intended to provide clarification
36. ANIMOSITY – strong feelings of dislike or hatred
37. ANNOTATE – to make notes to help explain or clarify
38. ANOMALY – deviation from the norm; atypical
39. ANTITHETICAL – characterized by extreme contrast
40. APPEASE – to make peace by giving into demands
41. APPRAISE – to assess the value or quality of something
42. APPROXIMATE – close but not completely accurate
43. AUGMENT – to increase
44. AUSTERE – very plain, without decoration

45. CATALYZE – to cause or speed up a reaction
46. CATASTROPHIC – utterly disastrous
47. CEASE – to stop, halt
48. CIRCUMVENT – to find a way around; avoid
49. CITE – to quote or reference from a work to support an argument
50. COALESCE – to come together to form a single mass
51. COARSENESS – roughness, harshness
52. COLLABORATION – the act of working with another person or people
53. COMMONPLACE – common, ordinary
54. COMPRISE – to include, contain
55. CONFINE – to restrict within a limited area
56. CONFOUND – to utterly confuse, baffle
57. CONSENSUS – general agreement
58. CONSPICUOUS – clearly visible; noticeable
59. CONSUMPTION – the process of eating or using up

60. CONTINGENT – dependent upon; subject to
61. CONTRIVE – to think up
62. COPIOUS – abundant; plentiful
63. CREDIBLE – believable
64. CREDULOUS – easily fooled

65. DEBACLE – a complete failure; fiasco
66. DEPLETE – to diminish
67. DESPONDENT – feeling depressed
68. DEVIATION – departure from what is normal
69. DEXTEROUS – physically skilled, especially with one's hands
70. DISCERNIBLE – visible; detectable
71. DISCORD – general disagreement
72. DISPARATE – very different
73. DISPERSE – to scatter
74. DISPOSITION – inherent personality or character trait
75. DIVERGE – to move apart
76. DOMESTICATION – the process of taming an animal or cultivating a wild plant
77. DRACONIAN – excessively harsh laws, rules, and punishments

78. ECCENTRIC – highly odd or unconventional (person)
79. ECLIPSE – to overshadow or block
80. ELICIT – to draw out, usually a response
81. ELUSIVE – difficult to find, catch, or achieve
82. ENGENDER – to cause or give rise to
83. ENGULF – to overwhelm; surround completely
84. ENHANCE – to improve or intensify
85. EPHEMERAL – very brief; short-lived
86. EQUITABLE – fair
87. ERRATIC – unpredictable; not regular
88. EVADE – to escape or avoid
89. EVINCE – to reveal or show one's feelings
90. EXACERBATE – to make worse
91. EXCAVATION – the process of digging up, usually a historic site
92. EXORBITANT – extreme and excessive
93. EXPLICIT – stated directly and with complete clarity
94. EXPLOIT – to take advantage of
95. EXPOSURE – contact with someone or something (noun form of "expose")

96. FABRICATE – to invent or make up, typically with the intent to deceive
97. FAÇADE – (false) exterior
98. FOSTER – to encourage or promote something typically seen to be good
99. FRUITFUL/FRUITLESS – productive/unproductive

100. GALVANIZE – to energize, spur into action

101. HAPHAZARD – random and disorganized
102. HETEROGENEOUS – varied, diverse; synonym for "multifaceted"
103. HINDER – to block, prevent; synonym for "impede"

104. IDEALIZE – to imagine something as better than it is in reality
105. IDIOSYNCRATIC – highly particular, unique to an individual
106. ILLUSORY – not real; based on an illusion
107. IMMINENT – about to happen
108. IMPEDE – to delay or prevent
109. IMPECCABLE – faultless, spotless
110. IMPENETRABLE – impossible to pass through
111. IMPERATIVE – of vital importance; crucial
112. IMPERCEPTIBLE – cannot be seen or perceived
113. IMPOSING – very large and impressive in appearance
114. IMPOVERISHED – very poor
115. INCONGRUOUS – out of place; something that contrasts with its surroundings
116. INDECIPHERABLE – unable to be read or understood
117. INDELIBLE – memorable; impossible to forget
118. INDIFFERENT – without interest or concern; apathetic
119. INDIGENOUS – native
120. INDOCTRINATE – to teach a person/people to uncritically accept beliefs
121. INDUCE – to persuade or influence someone to do something
122. INDULGENT – overly generous; too lenient
123. INELUCTABLE – inescapable; inevitable
124. INFALLIBLE – incapable of making mistakes
125. INFINITESIMAL – extremely small; approaching zero
126. INGENIOUS – very clever and cunning
127. INNOCUOUS – harmless; the synonym "benign" may also be used
128. INNOVATIVE – featuring new materials and ideas
129. INSIGHT – deep understanding
130. INSTALLATION – art exhibit consisting of large objects placed in a public space
131. INSUPERABLE – incapable of being overcome
132. INSURMOUNTABLE – too great to overcome
133. INTERMEDIATE - coming between two things
134. INTRICATE – very complex
135. INTRIGUING – arousing curiosity or interest
136. INTUITION – the ability to understand from an instinctive feeling
137. INVASIVE – spreading in a harmful manner (noun form of "invade")
138. IRATE – angry
139. IRREPROACHABLE – beyond criticism; faultless
140. IRREVOCABLE – permanent

141. JUXTAPOSITION – placement of two things next to each other for contrast

142. LACONIC – using few words; brief and to-the-point
143. LATENT – existing but in hidden or dormant form

144. LEGACY – a long-lasting impact
145. LINEAGE – descent from a common ancestor or predecessor
146. LUCRATIVE – very profitable

147. MANIFESTATION – visible appearance of an object, trend, or idea
148. MERCURIAL – unpredictable; constantly shifting moods
149. METICULOUS – very careful and precise; the synonym "punctilious" may also be used
150. MIGRATION – the movement of a person or group from one area to another
151. MISCONSTRUE – to misunderstand
152. MITIGATE – to make a problem less severe
153. MOBILIZE – to prepare a person or group for action
154. MOMENTOUS – having great significance (a decision or event)
155. MONETIZE – to make money from
156. MORIBUND – approaching death; on the verge of becoming obsolete
157. MULTIFACETED – having many aspects
158. MUNDANE – dull; uninteresting
159. MYRIAD – many

160. NEBULOUS – vague; undefined; synonym for "amorphous"
161. NEFARIOUS – wicked and evil
162. NUANCE – a subtle shade of difference or meaning
163. NURTURE – to care for and encourage growth and development

164. OBSCURE – rare; understood by few people
165. OFFHAND – done casually, without prior thought
166. OMINOUS – threatening; giving the impression that something bad will happen
167. ORIENTATION – a preference or liking for
168. ORTHODOX – conforming to a standard theory or belief
169. OVERLOAD – excessive burden or stress
170. OVERSHADOW – to dominate; make someone or something seem unimportant
171. OUTMODED – no longer fashionable; out of date
172. OUTSIZED – disproportionately large

173. PALPABLE – literally, touchable; often used to describe a very intense feeling
174. PAUCITY – a small or limited amount
175. PERIPHERAL – of secondary importance; not central
176. PERVASIVE – widespread
177. POLAR – very different; opposite
178. PRAGMATIC – practical
179. PRECIPITATE – to cause to happen especially suddenly and unexpectedly
180. PRECLUDE – prevent or block; synonym for "impede"
181. PRECURSOR – a person or thing that precedes; a forerunner
182. PREDATORY – preying upon others
183. PRESCIENT – showing great foresight
184. PRESCRIBE – to lay down a rule; dictate

185. PRETENTIOUS – affecting greater importance than one actually has
186. PRETEXT – false excuse given to justify a course of action
187. PREVAIL – to triumph over great odds
188. PRIORITIZE – to list or rate in order of importance
189. PRODIGIOUS – enormous; impressively large
190. PROFOUND – intellectually deep; extremely insightful
191. PROFUSION – large amount; synonym for "myriad"; antonym for "paucity"
192. PROHIBITIVE – so high (a difficulty or price) that it prevents something from occurring
193. PROLIFIC – very productive
194. PROVOCATIVE – causing a reaction, often annoyance or anger

195. RECANT – to take back; withdraw; renounce
196. RECIPROCATE – to respond to an action by doing the same thing back to someone
197. RECONCILE – to bring opposing people or things back together
198. REGISTER – (n.) official list or record; (v.) to become aware of or record
199. RELEVANT/IRRELEVANT – connected/unconnected to the topic at hand
200. RENOUNCE – to give up
201. REPLENISH – to refill; resupply
202. REPLICATE – to copy
203. RESILIENT – capable of quickly recovering from difficulty
204. RESURGENCE – the act of rising again into life or activity
205. RETROSPECT – hindsight; looking back
206. REVELATION – something that is revealed and thus made known
207. RUDIMENTARY – limited to basic principles; elementary

208. SABOTAGE – to deliberately destroy or damage
209. SATIATE – to fully satisfy
210. SCHEME – a clever and often devious plan
211. SCRUPULOUS – extremely attentive to details
212. SCRUTINIZE (n. SCRUTINY) – to examine very closely and carefully
213. SPECULATE – to form an explanation or theory; synonym for "conjecture"
214. SPURIOUS – false or fake; the synonym "specious" may also be used
215. STIPULATE – to demand or specify as part of an agreement
216. STRENUOUS – requiring great physical exertion
217. SUBJECTIVE – influenced by personal tastes, opinions, or feelings
218. SUBSTANTIAL – of considerable importance, size, or worth
219. SUPERFICIAL – shallow; lacking depth
220. SUPERFLUOUS – more than enough; unnecessary
221. SUPPLANT- to replace; supersede
222. SUPPLEMENT – (n.) an addition or reinforcement; (v.) to add on
223. SURPASS – to exceed; go beyond
224. SWAY – to persuade to follow a course of action
225. SYNCHRONIZE – to cause multiple events to occur at the same time
226. SYNOPSIS – a brief summary

227. TALLY – (n.) a recorded account; a total; (v.) to count
228. THWART – to block or get in the way of something negative
229. TRANSCEND – to rise above normal limitations
230. TEDIOUS – boring; dull and tiresome
231. TENUOUS – very weak; connected only slightly
232. TRIVIAL – unimportant

233. UBIQUITOUS – everywhere; synonym for "universal"
234. UNATTAINABLE – cannot be reached or achieved
235. UNCANNY – strange or slightly supernatural; beyond what is ordinary
236. UNCLASSIFIABLE – unable to be assigned to a category
237. UNCONVENTIONAL – not conforming to what is generally done or believed
238. UNDERMINE – to weaken; erode
239. UNDERSCORE – to emphasize by drawing attention to a fact, idea, or situation
240. UNEQUIVOCAL – leaving no doubt; certain
241. UNOBTRUSIVE – inconspicuous; not attracting attention
242. UNRESOLVABLE – unable to be resolved or settled
243. UNTENABLE – unable to be defended or supported

244. VACILLATE – to go back and forth between two options; synonym for "waver"
245. VALIDATE – to confirm the truth of a claim
246. VERISIMILITUDE – the quality of seeming to be true
247. VINDICATE – to free from blame; prove correct

248. WAIVE – to voluntarily give up the right to do something
249. WAVER – to go back and forth between two options; synonym for "vacillate"
250. WATERSHED – a turning point

CHAPTER 1
THE DSAT and 10 TOUGH WORDS

Advanced DSAT modules contain questions designed to test your understanding of challenging vocabulary words. This chapter defines and illustrates 10 words that often baffle students. Each word is then linked to a specific topic in Chapters 2–11.

1. **BARBIE ISN'T AS INNOCUOUS AS SHE SEEMS**
    * **INNOCUOUS – harmless; inoffensive**

With her perpetual smile and good-girl image, Barbie® is often viewed as bland and INNOCUOUS. When she was introduced in the 1950s, however, she represented a radical departure from the norm and ushered in a new era in American toys. Chapter 2 uses 10 more key DSAT vocabulary words to describe the past, present, and possible future of this surprisingly groundbreaking character.

2. **OPPENHEIMER'S DEEP AMBIVALANCE**
    * **AMBIVALENCE – mixed feelings**

Robert Oppenheimer had profoundly AMBIVALENT feelings about his role in creating the atomic bomb. As the widely acclaimed "father of the atomic bomb," he was intensely proud of his role in making the bomb and ending World War II. At the same time, however, he was painfully aware that the bomb could cause unprecedented death and destruction. Chapter 3 uses 10 more key DSAT vocabulary words to describe Oppenheimer and his role in the creation of the atomic bomb.

3. **THANOS'S TRIUMPH IS NOT INELUCTABLE**
   - **INELUCTABLE – inescapable, inevitable**

As the battle in the movie *Avengers: Endgame* reaches its final climax, Thanos defiantly boasts to a seemingly defeated Tony Stark that his victory cannot be avoided. But the evil warlord's triumph is not INELUCTABLE—the supervillain is defeated before he can destroy the universe. Chapter 4 uses 10 more key DSAT vocabulary words to explore classic and contemporary action movies and the heroes that have saved humanity.

4. **TAYLOR SWIFT IS UBIQUITOUS**
   - **UBIQUITOUS – everywhere at the same time; widespread**

Taylor Swift is UBIQUITOUS! The superstar is everywhere. Turn on the radio and there is a good chance you will hear a song from one of her best-selling albums. Her sold-out Eras Tour is performing before huge crowds in stadiums across America. Chapter 5 uses 10 key DSAT vocabulary words to describe Taylor's hit songs, performances, and fans.

5. **CONFOUNDED BY THE DEATH OF THE DINOSAURS**
   - **CONFOUND – totally confuse; baffle**

Dinosaurs dominated life on the planet for almost 200 million years. But they suddenly disappeared about 66 million years ago. What happened? Their mysterious extinction CONFOUNDED both scientists and a curious public. Chapter 6 uses 10 key DSAT science words to unravel how and why dinosaurs vanished.

6. **AN INNOVATIVE PROJECT**
   - **INNOVATIVE – new and groundbreaking**

Chapter 7 uses 10 key DSAT vocabulary words to tell the story of how a group of scientists from around the world used INNOVATIVE technology to alter the course of an asteroid … and perhaps save humanity from a fate similar to the dinosaurs'.

7. **DRACONIAN LAWS ARE REALLY STRICT**
   - **DRACONIAN – excessively harsh, e.g., laws, rules, and punishments**

Draco was an ancient Greek ruler whose code of laws called for very severe, or DRACONIAN, penalties for even the smallest offense. Draco would no doubt approve of the DRACONIAN laws imposed by President Snow in the *Hunger Games* trilogy. In *Catching Fire*, for example, Gale is almost whipped to death for illegally hunting outside the District 12 fence. Chapter 8 defines and illustrates the interesting histories of 10 key DSAT vocabulary words.

8. **WILL WASHINGTON PREVAIL?**
    - **PREVAIL – to win, triumph**

The American cause was very near collapse on Christmas night in 1776. Just five months had passed since overly confident colonists had proclaimed their independence from Great Britain. But during that time, Washington's army had suffered disastrous defeats and won no major victories. Many questioned Washington's leadership and openly wondered if the colonial cause could PREVAIL. Faced with a sense of great urgency, Washington boldly led his men across the Delaware River and surprised British forces in Trenton. His victory proved to be a pivotal event in American history. Chapter 9 uses 10 key DSAT vocabulary words to describe major events in American history.

9. **APPLE'S RESURGENCE**
    - **RESURGENCE – the act rising again into life or activity**

In 1977 Apple Computers was worth just $3 billion, and its stock sold for under $4 a share. Michael Dell and other tech leaders predicted that Apple would soon collapse. However, Steve Jobs launched the iPhone and a series of other innovative products that sparked a RESURGENCE in Apple's popularity and profits. The company's RESURGENCE continued in the years after Jobs's death in 2011. Today, Apple is worth over $3 trillion dollars. Chapter 10 uses RE- and other high-frequency prefixes to help you unlock the meaning of 10 key DSAT vocabulary words.

10. **AN EPICALLY WRONG (PRE-)SUPPOSITION**
    - **(PRE-)SUPPOSITION – assumption; something that is SUPPOSED**

Star Wars was perhaps the greatest sleeper hit ever to appear on the big screen. Executives at 20th Century Fox did not promote the film when it was released in 1977, considering it a high-risk project and supposing that it would not experience much success. However, their (PRE-)SUPPOSITION turned out to be radically incorrect. Although *Star Wars* initially played in only 32 theaters, word of mouth spread very quickly, and it went on to become the highest-grossing film of all time as well as a cultural sensation. Chapter 11 covers 10 key DSAT vocabulary words ending in the important suffix -TION.

CHAPTER 2

THE DSAT AND AN AMERICAN ICON

The release of the *Barbie* movie in the summer of 2023 thrust Mattel's iconic character into the spotlight. But where did she come from, and why did she become so popular? This chapter uses the history of this iconic character to define 10 must-know DSAT vocabulary words.

11. THE INVENTOR OF BARBIE® WAS AN ANOMALY
- **ANOMALY – deviation from the norm; atypical**

In the 1950s, when women made up only 30% of the American labor force and were typically restricted to teaching or secretarial work, Barbie's inventor, Ruth Handler, was an ANOMALY: a successful businesswoman, she and her husband co-founded the toy company Mattel, of which she served as president for several decades.

12. A PAUCITY OF ADULT-LOOKING DOLLS
- **PAUCITY – small amount; limited supply**

In the mid-1950s, virtually all the dolls sold in American markets were created to resemble infants. In other words, there was a notable PAUCITY of realistic dolls patterned after older children and adults. Handler became aware of this PAUCITY when she observed her young daughter, Barbara, assigning grownup roles to her paper dolls and discovered the gap in the doll market.

13. A MOMENTOUS ENCOUNTER
- **MOMENTOUS – having great significance (a decision or event)**

In 1956, Handler went on what would become a MOMENTOUS vacation. While traveling in Switzerland with Barbara and her son, Kenneth, she came across a doll called Bild Lilli. With its adult appearance, it was exactly what she had imagined would appeal to Barbara and other girls her age. Handler was thrilled; she bought three to bring back to the United States.

14. THE POLAR OPPOSITE OF AMERICAN DOLLS
- **POLAR – very different, opposing**

Bild Lilli, which was produced in Germany, was the POLAR opposite of the baby dolls found in American toy stores. Based on a popular comic-strip character, she sported a trim figure and came with a fashionable wardrobe. Although she had not been conceived of as a children's product, she proved to be very popular with young girls, who enjoyed dressing her in various outfits.

15. AN UNCONVENTIONAL PRODUCT
- **UNCONVENTIONAL – different from what is normal**

When Handler returned to California, she enlisted the help of a local inventor who helped her redesign Bild Lilli to match her vision. She also gave her creation a new name: Barbie®, after her daughter. Handler was enthusiastic about the doll's prospects; however, market analysts considered the "teen-age fashion model" too UNCONVENTIONAL for American buyers, who were accustomed to infants, and predicted that it would sell poorly. They were quickly proven wrong, though: Barbie's very UNCONVENTIONALITY held great appeal. More than 300,000 dolls were sold the first year, and sales grew rapidly thereafter.

16. IS BARBIE CATASTROPHIC FOR THE ENVIRONMENT?
- **CATASTROPHIC – disastrous**

Although Mattel has given its signature product an environmentalist twist by releasing the Barbie Eco-Leadership Team™, the fact remains that Barbie is made of plastic. Nearly 60 million dolls have been sold each year since 1959, so more than 1 billion Barbies have been sold overall, and each one can take hundreds of years to break down in a landfill. Although Mattel's buy-back-recycling program is designed to prevent its products from having a CATASTROPHIC impact on the environment, only about 9% of its toys are currently recycled.

17. BARBIE'S PROFOUND DESPAIR
- **PROFOUND – intellectually deep; extremely insightful**

Given Barbie's somewhat vacant expression and impossibly perfect Southern California lifestyle, PROFOUND was not a word typically associated with the doll—until the summer of 2023, that is. The film *Barbie* derives much of its humor from the contrast between the character's stereotypical image and her sudden awareness of her own mortality. As she ponders the meaning of her seemingly perfect life, Barbie's existential crisis is PROFOUND.

18. **A FEW CRITICS FIND *BARBIE* TEDIOUS**
    - **TEDIOUS – boring; dull and tiresome**

On the whole, the *Barbie* film received glowing reviews for its novel treatment of a well-known character; however, some viewers found the movie TEDIOUS and superficial, considering its depiction of Barbie Land's endless perfection dull and repetitive. Writing in the *New York Post*, Johnny Oleksinski described the film as having packaging that was "a lot more fun than the TEDIOUS toy inside the box." Ouch!

19. **BARBIE AND DOROTHY – A POSSIBLE ANALOGY**
    - **ANALOGY – a comparison intended to provide clarification**

Happily for Mattel, most film critics reacted far more positively to *Barbie* than Oleksinski. Still, it is fair to wonder: is there a deeper meaning underlying Barbie's seemingly random real-world experiences? An important clue can be found in the movie's opening scene as Barbie drives past a movie theater. Outside posters indicate that *The Wizard of Oz* is playing on the big screen inside. Is this a coincidence? Or does it provide viewers with an insightful ANALOGY? Like Dorothy, Barbie is in a new world where she embarks upon a journey of self-discovery. This ANALOGY signals a thematic link that Barbie is more than an entertaining movie with catchy songs and striking sets; it is also a thought-provoking story about a character's search for identity.

20. **MATTEL WILL CONTINUE TO MONETIZE BARBIE**
    - **MONETIZE – to make money from**

Today, Barbie is Mattel's most profitable and important product. The company sells 58 million dolls every year to people in 150 countries around the world. With the release of the $140 million *Barbie* movie, Mattel hopes to further MONETIZE its iconic doll by sparking additional sales and by generating enthusiasm for a long list of toy and movie tie-ins that are already in the works.

CHAPTER 3

THE DSAT, J. ROBERT OPPENHEIMER, AND THE ATOMIC BOMB

The Pulitzer Prize-winning book *American Prometheus: The Triumph and Tragedy of Robert Oppenheimer* by Kai Bird and Martin J. Sherwin, and the movie *Oppenheimer* directed by Christopher Nolan, tell the fascinating, controversial, and poignant story of why and how the United States created an atomic bomb. This chapter uses 10 key words to illustrate the dramatic events surrounding the origins and testing of the atomic bomb.

21.   **A WORLD ENGULFED IN WAR**
- **ENGULF – to overwhelm; surround completely**

World War II began on September 1, 1939, when Hitler's army launched a blitzkrieg attack on Poland. Within two years, war ENGULFED the entire globe as conflict raged across Europe and the Pacific.

22.   **AN OMINOUS DEVELOPMENT**
- **OMINOUS – threatening; giving the impression that something bad will happen**

OMINOUS reports from Europe indicated that German scientists had successfully learned how to split a uranium atom. Fears soon arose that Hitler could use nuclear fission to build an immensely powerful atomic bomb that would pose a grave threat to Europe and America.

23. GALVANIZED INTO ACTION
  - **GALVANIZE – to energize; to spur into action**

No one knew how close the Nazis were to developing an atomic bomb. But this threat GALVANIZED the Roosevelt administration into action. In August 1942, the United States launched the Manhattan Project: a top-secret program to build and test an atomic bomb.

24. A PRODIGIOUS EFFORT
  - **PRODIGIOUS – enormous, impressively large**

The Manhattan Project represented a PRODIGIOUS investment in resources to win the nuclear arms race against Nazi Germany. Given unlimited funding, the Manhattan Project's budget swelled to over $2 billion (equal to $24 billion in 2023 dollars) and involved the labor of some 500,000 people, nearly 1% of the entire U.S. civilian labor force.

25. A SUCCESSFUL COLLABORATION
  - **COLLABORATION – the act of working with another person or people**

An atomic bomb could not build itself. To succeed, the Manhattan Project required the COLLABORATION of gifted administrators. In September 1942, the Roosevelt administration chose Major General Leslie Groves to direct the Manhattan Project. Groves had previously distinguished himself as a successful engineer who got results. He then surprised his staff by selecting J. Robert Oppenheimer as the Scientific Director of the Los Alamos National Laboratory. Although Oppenheimer had no previous administrative experience, Groves recognized him as a brilliant and charming scientist who had a gift for understanding and explaining complex topics.

26. A VERY INTRICATE "GADGET"
  - **INTRICATE – very complex and detailed**

Oppenheimer and his team of top scientists worked tirelessly to resolve scientific questions and create a bomb. The finished bomb was shaped like a large steel globe. Code-named "Gadget," the bomb included an INTRICATE array of highly refined components. For example, tons of specially fitted high-explosive wedges encased a solid sphere of plutonium. When detonated, they would focus a perfectly timed blast wave on the ball of plutonium.

27. LOOKING FOR AN UNEQUIVOCAL ANSWER
- **UNEQUIVOCAL – leaving no doubt, certain**

In the movie *Oppenheimer*, General Groves is justifiably worried that "Gadget" could release enough energy to ignite the atmosphere and destroy the world. Oppenheimer responds by calmly telling Groves that the possibility of that occurring is almost zero. But this is not the UNEQUIVOCAL answer Groves is looking for. Unnerved by the thought of destroying humanity, he replies that zero would be preferable.

28. PALPABLE TENSION
- **PALPABLE – literally, touchable; often used to describe a very intense feeling**

After more than two years of intense work, Oppenheimer and his staff felt a PALPABLE sense of hope and dread. As the countdown proceeded, seconds seemed like hours. Questions filled everyone's mind: What if the test failed? But what if it worked and ignited the atmosphere? No one knew the answer.

29. SURPASSING ALL EXPECTATIONS
- **SURPASS – to exceed; go beyond**

"Gadget" successfully detonated at 5:30 a.m. on July 16, 1945. The explosive force of the bomb SURPASSED all expectations. Oppenheimer had predicted that the bomb might be equivalent to 5,000 tons of TNT. Instead, the bomb exploded with the force of approximately 20,000 tons of TNT.

30. A WATERSHED MOMENT
- **WATERSHED – a critical turning point**

The golden, purple, violet, gray, and blue mushroom-shaped cloud that rose over the New Mexico desert marked a WATERSHED moment in human history. The United States now had a weapon that would soon end World War II. But within a short time, a Cold War broke out between the United States and the Soviet Union. These two superpowers promptly launched a dangerous and expensive nuclear arms race that had the potential to destroy civilization.

CHAPTER 4
THE DSAT GOES TO THE MOVIES

Since the dawn of Hollywood, action movies have been some of the film industry's most reliable blockbusters, racking up billions of dollars at the box office and attracting legions of dedicated fans. This chapter uses a variety of classic and contemporary action films to illustrate 10 top DSAT words.

31.   AN ENDURING LEGACY
  - **LEGACY – a long-lasting impact**

Released in 1903 by the Edison Manufacturing Company, *The Great Train Robbery* is generally considered the first action movie. Although it was just 12 minutes long, the film left a LEGACY of production techniques such as on-location shooting and frequent camera movement, which were quickly adopted by other directors. The first blockbuster, it also continued to be referenced in numerous film and television shows for decades to come.

32.   KING KONG IS IMPOSING
  - **IMPOSING – very large and impressive in appearance**

From their beginnings, action movies have relied on improbably large and IMPOSING fictional creations that their heroes must battle to save the world. In 1933, for example, the first King Kong movie featured the IMPOSING gorilla, who towered over New York City and climbed to the top of the Empire State Building. Another, even more IMPOSING movie creation was Godzilla, who in the 2014 film bearing his name was intended to measure 355 feet.

33. SABOTAGE IN THE SPACE RACE
- **SABOTAGE** – to deliberately destroy or damage; n., deliberate destruction or damage

Sabotage is a common staple of action and spy movies, including the first James Bond film, *Dr. No* (1962). Produced during the Cold War, when anxieties over the space race were running high, the plot centers on the evil Dr. No's attempts to SABOTAGE the American Space program with a special radio beam. Bond—played by film icon Sean Connery—is sent to Jamaica to investigate the murder of a Secret Intelligence Service agent, where he eventually discovers Dr. No's lair. Will Bond stop the villain and his henchmen? Of course! Dr. No's attempt at SABOTAGE is thwarted, and the Space Shuttle Mercury lifts off.

34. AN INGENIOUS PLAN
- **INGENIOUS** – very clever

In addition to the exploits of the master spy himself, the James Bond films also include a character known as Q, or Quartermaster. Responsible for secret field technologies, Q creates INGENIOUS inventions such as toothpaste bombs. The character may have been based on a World War I veteran named Christopher Hutton, who produced a variety of regular-looking objects that could be used in INGENIOUS ways. For example, he used magnetized pencil clips, razor blades, and fountain pens to create miniature compasses for army pilots.

35. THE PAST IS NOT IRREVOCABLE
- **IRREVOCABLE** – unable to be changed or undone

How might the world be different if people could go back in time and change the past? That question formed the premise of the hit *Terminator* films: set in the late twentieth century and 2029, they depict an alternate reality in which super-intelligent robots have taken over the world and attempted to eliminate humanity. However, this situation is not IRREVOCABLE! In *Terminator 2*, the laboratory housing the destructive technology is destroyed. The past can be changed after all.

36. IT'S ALL CONTINGENT ON THE DINOSAURS
- **CONTINGENT** – dependent on; subject to

Like the *Terminator* franchise, which exploited special effects for maximum impact, the *Jurassic Park* films revolved around creatures generated by computer. In fact, the movies' chance of success was entirely CONTINGENT on the convincing appearance and movement of these non-existent animals— if they did not appear realistic, and terrifying, the films would flop. Luckily, special-effects creator Stan Winston was able to work his magic, allowing the visuals to stand the test of time.

37. **AN INFINITESIMAL CHANCE OF SUCCESS**
   - **INFINITESIMAL – extremely small; approaching zero**

Considered one of the greatest films ever made, Steven Spielberg's 1998 smash-hit *Saving Private Ryan* tells the story of a rescue mission that has only an INFINITESIMAL chance of success: a group of soldiers must navigate the chaos of post-D-Day France to locate a soldier and bring him home to his family. Without a clear plan and with little information to help them identify their target, this is truly a daunting task! Nevertheless, they overcome the INFINITESIMAL odds and succeed in finding Private Ryan.

38. **AN EPIC BUT HAPHAZARD BATTLE**
   - **HAPHAZARD – random and disorganized**

In the Bourne franchise, which features Matt Damon as a CIA operative suffering from amnesia, director Paul Greengrass frequently employs what appears to be a HAPHAZARD camera style: the focus changes rapidly, alternating between broad shots and close-ups to create a sense of chaos. However, as critic Peter Suderman pointed out in an article for *Vox* magazine, this HAPHAZARD quality is only an illusion: in reality, each shot is carefully selected to convey important plot information.

39. **FROM PERIPHERAL TO VITAL**
   - **PERIPHERAL – of secondary importance; not central**

Over the course of *The Dark Night* Batman trilogy, Lucius Fox evolves from a PERIPHERAL player to a central character. Portrayed by veteran actor Morgan Freeman, Fox quickly becomes one of the few people to discover that Batman is actually Bruce Wayne. While he acts mostly as a technical assistant during the first film, he is essentially overseeing Wayne Enterprises by the third installment and is PERIPHERAL no more.

40. **A MULTIFACETED GROUP OF SUPERHEROES**
   - **MULTIFACETED – having many aspects**

In the *Avengers* series, the title characters are a group of superheroes who possess a MULTIFACETED array of skills and superhuman powers. For example, Thor is the God of Thunder and wields a powerful hammer. Bruce Banner is a renowned physicist who, after a failed experiment with gamma radiation, transforms into the Hulk, a huge muscular creature with green skin. And Tony Stark is a billionaire genius who invents a suit of armor that gives him extraordinary strength and an arsenal of potent weapons. Known as "Earth's Mightiest Heroes," this MULTIFACETED team often joins with other superheroes to defeat villains who threaten life on Earth.

CHAPTER 5

THE DSAT, TAYLOR SWIFT,
AND THE ERAS TOUR

Taylor Swift's Eras Tour (March 2023-December 2024) has become a defining pop culture event. This chapter uses 10 DSAT vocabulary words to describe everything from the EXORBITANT cost of tickets to Taylor's METICULOUS costumes.

41.   EXORBITANT TICKET PRICES
   - **EXORBITANT – extreme and excessive (price)**

How much would you be willing to pay for seats to attend one of Taylor Swift's Eras Tour performances? One fan purchased six tickets for $1,519, or $253 each. The seats had a clear view of the stage. A few months later, StubHub offered comparable seats for $2,000 each. Would you have paid this price? Or would you have considered it EXORBITANT? EXORBITANT literally means "out of orbit." The loyal fan refused to sell her prized tickets saying, "The ticket prices are outrageous, but the experience is priceless."

42.   IS THERE ANY WAY TO MITIGATE EXORBITANT CONCERT PRICES?
   - **MITIGATE – to make a problem less severe**

Can anything be done to MITIGATE the soaring prices to popular concerts such as Taylor Swift's Eras Tour? The short answer is probably not. Ticket prices are a function of supply and demand. When the demand for tickets far exceeds the supply, prices will rise. Experts recommend that fans MITIGATE the problem by avoiding scammers and purchasing tickets with secure payment methods.

43. METICULOUS BODYSUITS AND GOWNS
- **METICULOUS – very careful and precise**

Taylor's three-hour-and-15-minute concerts are divided into sections, each representing one of her 10 albums. It is thus a journey through the musical eras that define Swift's almost two-decade-long career. During her performances, Swift wears a series of 16 METICULOUSLY designed bodysuits and gowns that represent her albums. For example, she opens the show wearing a suit adorned with pink and blue jewels that reflect the dreamy sky on the cover of her *Lover* album. Later in the concert a beautiful lilac gown recalls the mood of the songs in her *Folklore* album.

44. MANDATORY SONGS
- **MANDATORY – required; obligatory**

Taylor has over 200 songs she can use to create the setlist for her Eras Tour concert. Narrowing this massive body of work down to just 44 songs represents a formidable task. As expected, the final setlist includes a number of MANDATORY fan favorites, along with tracks that mark milestones in her incredible career.

45. ANTITHETICAL RIVALS
- **ANTITHETICAL – characterized by an extreme contrast**

In her song "You Belong with Me," Taylor draws a sharp contrast between herself and a popular, rival girl who serves as Cheer Captain while Taylor sits on the sidelines. And to make the contrast even greater, Taylor's rival wears very feminine clothing in contrast to Taylor's more casual attire. In short, the two girls have totally ANTITHETICAL looks and personalities.

46. TAYLOR'S AFFINITY FOR A MYSTERY MAN (HARRY STYLES?)
- **AFFINITY – a strong attraction or liking**

Taylor is unable to overcome the advantages of her rival in "You Belong with Me." But no matter. In her song "Style," Taylor and an unnamed lover (allegedly Harry Styles) share a strong physical AFFINITY for each other. Taylor describes their AFFINITY, comparing the mystery man to a daydreamy James Dean and invoking the classic appeal of her red lips. Given this physical AFFINITY, the two will stay in style forever.

47. KATY PERRY ENGENDERS CONFLICT
- **ENGENDER – to cause or give rise to**

Taylor Swift's songs often describe a failed relationship with an ex-boyfriend. But her song "Bad Blood" describes her deep anger toward A-List singer Katy Perry. Swift doesn't pull any punches when she accuses Perry of causing a rupture between them. What did Perry do to ENGENDER this conflict? Taylor believes that Perry tried to sabotage an entire arena tour by luring away some of her key backup dancers. In addition, Perry dared to date John Mayer, one of Taylor's ex-boyfriends. Taylor concludes that Perry's thoughtless actions have ENGENDERED hurt feelings, with lasting scars.

48. TAYLOR IGNORES CRITICAL SCRUTINY
- **SCRUTINY – critical examination (v., SCRUTINIZE)**

Taylor's rise to stardom has attracted close media SCRUTINY of her personal life and especially her image as a flirt with numerous romantic attachments. In her song "Shake it Off," Taylor acknowledges that she goes out on too many dates. However, she also implies that she's a "player" who does what she wants to do. And at the same, she acknowledges that some people will dislike her regardless of how she behaves. Taylor has finally learned to live with the public SCRUTINY that comes with being a superstar. Her new confident attitude toward unfair criticism is to let it roll off her back.

49. FANTASTICALLY LUCRATIVE
- **LUCRATIVE – very profitable**

Taylor's open and relatable songs about teenage heartbreak have won her the loyalty of millions of fans known as "Swifties." An estimated 14 million fans attempted to buy tickets to her sold out Eras Tour. The tour is proving to be extremely LUCRATIVE. Forbes Magazine estimates that Taylor is earning around $13.9 million for each performance. She could become a billionaire when The Eras Tour ends in August 2024.

50. AN OUTSIZED ECONOMIC IMPACT
- **OUTSIZED – disproportionately large**

Taylor Swift's Eras Tour is doing more than making her fabulously wealthy; it is also having an OUTSIZED economic impact on the cities where she performs. For example, a nationwide survey by QuestionPro revealed that Taylor Swift concert-goers are spending more than $1,000 per event on tickets, food, hotel rooms, and merchandise. Taylor has thus become a welcome and OUTSIZED economic stimulus package for the cities she visits.

CHAPTER 6

THE DSAT AND THE DEMISE OF
THE DINOSAURS

Scientific terms such as CONJECTURE and SKEPTICS make frequent appearances on DSAT questions. The sudden extinction of the dinosaurs provides a fascinating and sometimes controversial story that illustrates these key words.

51.   DINOSAURS WERE A PERVASIVE PRESENCE
- **PERVASIVE – widespread**

About 66 million years ago lush vegetation and dense forests covered much of the Earth's surface and supported a huge variety of life. Dinosaurs were a PERVASIVE presence throughout the globe. At that time, they had diversified into hundreds of species of all shapes and sizes. Their reign as Earth's largest and most powerful animals seemed destined to last for millions more years.

52.   AN ABRUPT END
- **ABRUPT – sudden and unexpected**

The dinosaurs' reign came to an ABRUPT end. Within a relatively short time, dinosaurs, along with 75 percent of all plant and animal species, vanished. What caused this ABRUPT mass extinction?

53. A TENUOUS LINK
- **TENUOUS – very weak, slight**

The sudden disappearance of the dinosaurs has long fascinated and puzzled scientists and the general public. But convincing answers proved difficult to find. One leading theory pointed to a supernova as the probable culprit. A supernova occurs when a star explodes. A supernova near Earth could damage the planet's atmosphere, causing mass extinctions. However, astronomers haven't located a dangerous supernova near Earth. As a result, the link between a supernova and the sudden disappearance of the dinosaurs is TENUOUS at best.

54. A CONTROVERSIAL CONJECTURE
- **CONJECTURE – n., hypothesis; v., to hypothesize**

The disappearance of the dinosaurs intrigued geologist Walter Alvarez and his father, Nobel Prize-winning physicist Luis Alvarez. They noticed the presence of unusual quantities of iridium at sites dating to 66 million years ago. Iridium is a very dense metal that is one of the rarest elements on the Earth's surface. However, iridium is found in asteroids in much larger quantities. In 1980, the Alvarezes published a controversial CONJECTURE in which they speculated that a massive asteroid had struck the planet and caused the extinction of the dinosaurs.

55. CORROBORATING EVIDENCE
- **CORROBORATE – to confirm or support a statement or claim**

In February 1990, a team of North American researchers confirmed the discovery of a massive impact crater just off the coast of Mexico's Yucatan Peninsula. Although the crater is not visible from the surface, geologists have confirmed that it is 111 to 125 miles in diameter and that it was formed when an asteroid slammed into the Earth 66 million years ago. The crater's size and age provided persuasive evidence that appeared to CORROBORATE the Alvarez's controversial CONJECTURE.

56. A CALAMITOUS COLLISION
- **CALAMITOUS – extremely disastrous**

Scientists now believe that a six-mile-wide asteroid the size of Mount Everest crashed into the Earth 66 million years ago. The impact released an amount of energy equivalent to 100,000,000 tons of TNT, or over a billion times the energy of the atomic bombs dropped on Hiroshima and Nagasaki. This CALAMITOUS collision would have unleashed a devastating combination of continent-shaking earthquakes, gigantic uncontrolled fires, and a suffocating darkness that transformed the Earth into a desolate planet devoid of most life.

57. DR. KELLER SURMISES A DIFFERENT EXPLANATION
- **SURMISE – to assume; draw a conclusion without strong evidence**

The discovery of a massive impact crater in shallow water adjacent to the Yucatan Peninsula seemed to offer strong support for the Alvarezes CONJECTURE. However, Dr. Gerta Keller, a Professor of Geosciences at Princeton University, wasn't convinced. She acknowledged that the impact theory was "a fantastic idea." But she also asked, "Is it true?" Dr. Keller then offered an alternative explanation. Based on geologic samples from India's Deccan Plateau, which showed a progressive disappearance of life after massive volcanic eruptions shook the region approximately 65 million years ago, she SURMISED that the eruptions had been responsible for the mass extinctions.

58. DR. KELLER CHALLENGES HER SKEPTICS
- **SKEPTIC – doubter; disbeliever (adj. – SKEPTICAL)**

Dr. Keller recognized that overcoming the opposition of SKEPTICS would be a challenge. She began by pointing out that the asteroid had actually struck the Earth about 100,000 years before the onset of the great extinction. She also stressed that volcanic eruptions in India released huge quantities of greenhouse gases such as carbon dioxide, sulphur dioxide, and chlorine into the atmosphere. Over time, these poisonous gases suffocated wildlife and caused the food chain to collapse.

59. PROPONENTS REACH A MIDDLE GROUND
- **PROPONENT – a person who supports a theory, proposal, or project**

PROPONENTS of both the asteroid-impact and volcanic-eruption theories published numerous scholarly articles defending their respective points of view. However, new research suggests that a combination of these two phenomena may have created a "double-punch" that caused the mass extinction of the dinosaurs and other plant and animal species. PROPONENTS of this middle ground appear to be gaining more and more support.

60. ADVANTAGEOUS FOR SMALLER MAMMALS
- **ADVANTAGEOUS – creating favorable circumstances**

The mass extinction of the dinosaurs proved to be ADVANTAGEOUS for smaller mammals. Over time, new generations of elephants, lions, and bison became the dominant species. And after many millions of years, Earth's new environment proved ADVANTAGEOUS for the first Homo Sapiens.

CHAPTER 7

THE DSAT AND THE DART MISSION

The asteroid that crashed into the Earth 66 million years ago wasn't the first such body on a collision course with our planet, and it won't be the last either. But luckily, some impressive new tools have been developed since then. This chapter uses an additional 10 DSAT words to describe a daring recent mission to help humanity avoid the dinosaurs' fate.

61. INDELIBLE IMAGES
- **INDELIBLE – unable to be removed or forgotten**

Although the asteroid responsible for the dinosaurs' extinction crashed into the Earth millions of years ago, artists' renderings and electronically generated images of an immense fiery mass plummeting into the Earth while dinosaurs peacefully basked in the sun have made an INDELIBLE impression—one that reminds people of Earth's vulnerability and is impossible to forget.

62. YOU CAN'T BE INDIFFERENT ABOUT AN ASTEROID
- **INDIFFERENT – uninterested; not caring**

Scientists knew that if a similar asteroid were to collide with the Earth today, its effects would be similarly dire. Although risk of a catastrophic asteroid impact was small, humanity could not afford to remain INDIFFERENT! In fact, about 40% of asteroids as wide as 500 feet could pose a threat to the Earth. In 2015, researchers at NASA and the European Space Agency began to develop a joint plan to alter the orbit of one of these bodies while it was still far away in space.

63. ARE THE OBSTACLES INSURMOUNTABLE?
- **INSURMOUNTABLE – too difficult to be overcome**

At first, critics of the plan appear to have a point: the obstacles to such a task appeared INSURMOUNTABLE. Any asteroid that threatened Earth would be not only enormous but also made of solid rock. Furthermore, it would be whizzing through space at an extremely high speed. To make matters even more complicated, asteroids come in many different shapes and have a wide range of surface properties and internal structures.

64. A CLEVER SCHEME TO SAVE HUMANITY
- **SCHEME – a clever and often devious plan**

Engineers devised a clever and audacious (very bold) SCHEME. Dubbed DART—Double Asteroid Redirection Test—it was referred to by the U.S. Space Agency as the first planetary defense test. The project involved directing a specially built spacecraft to crash into an asteroid at very high speed. The force of the collision would be so great that it would alter the asteroid's orbit.

65. DIVERGENT VIEWS ABOUT THE MISSION
- **DIVERGENT – differing, opposing**

The extreme boldness of the scheme led to DIVERGENT views about its prospects for success. While the scientists involved in DART were confident in their ability to reroute an asteroid, some critics of the project believed that a spacecraft would not be strong enough to knock such a large object off-course.

66. SCIENTISTS REMAIN ADAMANT
- **ADAMANT – extremely stubborn or insistent**

Despite the obstacles they faced, scientists remained ADAMANT that their plan could succeed. After months of searching, they identified the asteroid Dimorphos as a prime target for redirection. Although it did not threaten the Earth, it had other characteristics that made it an ideal test case. In addition to being less than 500 feet across, Dimorphos orbited a larger asteroid, passing both in front of it and behind it. As a result, telescopes on Earth could easily measure variations in brightness to track its orbit. The impact was planned for the fall of 2022, when Dimorphos would be at its closest point to Earth—"only" 6.8 million miles—in order to enable the highest quality of observations.

67. THE DART MISSION USES INNOVATIVE TECHNOLOGY
- **INNOVATIVE – new and groundbreaking**

The DART project relied on INNOVATIVE kinetic impact technologies. Measuring approximately 4 x 4.5 x 4.5 feet, the spacecraft itself was remarkably compact and weighed just under 1,350 lbs. It also featured two large solar arrays as well as a cube equipped with cameras that could capture both wide- and narrow-frame images of the asteroid's rocky surface as the spacecraft approached for the collision.

68. FOSTERING A SENSE OF COLLABORATION
- **FOSTER – to encourage or promote (something good)**

Because it addressed a matter of planetary concern, the DART project was designed to FOSTER international collaboration. Although it was directed by a team at John Hopkins University in Baltimore and run by NASA, participants came from countries all over the world, including France, Japan, Peru, and South Korea.

69. WILL THE DART MISSION BECOME A DEBACLE?
- **DEBACLE (deh-BAH-kul) – a complete failure; fiasco**

Would the innovative scheme succeed, or would the whole thing turn into a DEBACLE? Less than a year after its launch, at 7:14 p.m. on September 26th, 2022, the DART craft met its asteroid target. At mission control at Laurel, Maryland, the room erupted in cheers as mission systems engineer Elena Adams announced the ship's impact with Dimorphos.

70. EXPOSURE TO DEEP SPACE MAKES THE ASTEROID BLUE
- **EXPOSURE – the state of being exposed**

When the spacecraft blasted through the asteroid, the impact blew more than 1 million pounds (2.2 million kilograms) off its mass and formed a tail that stretched for thousands of miles. It also revealed the asteroid's rocky center; the EXPOSURE to space made it temporarily appear blue to the scientists observing the aftermath of the collision. A little over two weeks later, data analysis confirmed that the asteroid's orbit had been altered by 32 minutes as a result of the collision. The project was a success!

CHAPTER 8

THE DSAT AND WORDS WITH A HISTORY

Every English word has a history. In this chapter, we travel back and forth in time, presenting DSAT words that tell interesting stories. Hopefully, you will find these word histories both interesting and memorable!

71.   **TRIVIAL CHATTER IN ANCIENT ROME**
- **TRIVIAL – unimportant**

TRIVIAL derives from the Latin words *tri*, meaning "three," and *via*, meaning "road." In ancient Rome, TRIVIAL literally referred to a place where three roads met. Remember, the ancient Romans did not have cars or motorcycles. Most people traveled on foot. At three-way intersections pedestrians often paused to exchange small talk about their everyday lives. TRIVIAL thus came to mean "of little importance, insignificant."

72.   **MYRIAD MYRIAD IS TOO BIG TO IMAGINE**
- **MYRIAD – Many**

MYRIAD is actually an ancient Greek word meaning "ten thousand." The largest number the ancient Greeks could imagine was MYRIAD MYRIAD, or 10,000 times 10,000! It is interesting to note that both centipedes and millipedes are arthropods (types of insects) that have a large, or MYRIAD, number of legs. That is why they belong to the subphylum *Myriapoda*!

73. COPIOUS IS OVERFLOWING WITH ABUNDANCE
- **COPIOUS – abundant, plentiful**

After the June 2023 International DSAT, a student reported that they had "got stuck on the word COPIOUS." Since they did not know the meaning of this word, they guessed that it had something to do with copying. Wrong! COPIOUS is actually derived from the Latin word *copia*, meaning "abundant." For example, students often take COPIOUS notes as they prepare for AP® exams.

74. EPHEMERAL IS HERE TODAY AND GONE TOMORROW
- **EPHEMERAL – very brief; short-lived**

EPHEMERAL is both a beautiful and a sad word. It is derived from the Greek word *hemera*, meaning "a day." EPHEMERAL reminds us that we should "seize the day" and treasure the beautiful moments in our lives. For example, rainbows are both beautiful and EPHEMERAL.

75. NEFARIOUS VILLIANS ARE VERY BAD
- **NEFARIOUS – wicked and evil**

Wicked people have unfortunately been a part of society since the dawn of history. In ancient Rome, the Latin word *nefarius* referred to a criminal. The word NEFARIOUS is now used to describe a person who is extremely evil. The Wicked Witch of the West (*Wizard of Oz)*, Bellatrix Lestrange (*Harry Potter*), and Darth Vader (*Star Wars*) are all iconic and NEFARIOUS villains.

76. LACONIC GETS TO THE POINT
- **LACONIC – using few words; brief and to-the-point**

The ancient Spartans were renowned warriors who lived in a region of Greece called Laconia. They valued deeds far more than words. As a result, the Spartans became famous for their concise, or LACONIC, diplomatic messages. When the powerful conqueror Philip of Macedon invaded Greece, he sent the Spartans a message asking if they wanted him to come as a friend or a foe. The Spartans upheld their reputation for LACONIC replies when they answered, "Neither!"

77. MORIBUND IS BAD FOR BUSINESS
- **MORIBUND – approaching death; on the verge of becoming obsolete**

What do Blockbuster, Toys "R" Us, and Borders Books all have in common? They were all visited by Mors, the cold and merciless Roman god of death (although Toys "R" Us was revived the year after its stores closed). Mors' name continues to live in the DSAT word MORIBUND. A product or company that is MORIBUND has been visited by Mors and is doomed!

78. DEXTEROUS PEOPLE ARE GOOD WITH THEIR HANDS
- **DEXTEROUS – physically skilled, especially with one's hands**

The Latin word *dexter* means "right hand." Since the ancient Romans believed that right-handed people had more manual skill than left-handed people, the word DEXTEROUS came to mean "very skillful." This long-standing bias can still be seen in the word DEXTEROUS. For example, being DEXTEROUS is an essential trait for magicians!

79. ARE YOU A PROLIFIC TIKTOK POSTER?
- **PROLIFIC – very productive**

What do Charli D'Amelio, Bella Poarch, and Addison Rae have in common? They are all super PROLIFIC and popular TikTok posters. Although they are very proud of their TikTok status, these PROLIFIC posters probably do not know that PROLIFIC is derived from the Latin word *proles* meaning children. Ancient Romans valued PROLIFIC mothers just as modern Internet users value PROLIFIC TikTok posters.

80. MERCURIAL WON'T STAND STILL
- **MERCURIAL – unpredictable; constantly shifting moods**

In ancient mythology, Mercury was the messenger of the gods who flew with the aid of his winged sandals. Mercury was active, swift, and above all changeable. Today, MERCURIAL is used to describe a person who is born under the planet Mercury and is thus unpredictable and given to rapidly shifting moods. For example, Miley Cyrus is a MERCURIAL singer and songwriter whose quickly evolving moods have given her fans and critics plenty to talk about.

CHAPTER 9
THE DSAT AND AMERICAN HISTORY

The sinking of the warship *Maine*, the Stock Market Crash of 1929, and Rosa Parks's refusal to give up her seat are all famous events in American history. But what do they have to do with the DSAT? This chapter uses these and other famous events to illustrate 10 words commonly found on the DSAT.

81. A PRESCIENT PREDICTION
- **PRESCIENT – showing great foresight**

The Missouri Compromise of 1820 temporarily defused the political crisis over the expansion of slavery. However, the settlement foreshadowed the increasingly bitter sectional struggles that lay ahead. Thomas Jefferson sensed the future peril when he PRESCIENTLY wrote, "This momentous question, like a fire bell in the night, awakened and filled me with terror ... It is hushed for the moment, but this is a reprieve only."

82. A FAILED ATTEMPT TO IMPEDE PROGRESS
- **IMPEDE - to delay or block; hinder**

The Seneca Falls Convention in 1848 marked the beginning of a long and frustrating battle for women's suffrage. Opponents IMPEDED the women's suffrage movement by claiming that women were a "weaker sex" who should avoid public affairs and confine themselves to their domestic roles as wives and mothers. These efforts to IMPEDE progress ultimately failed. In 1920, the states ratified the Nineteenth Amendment granting women the right to vote.

83. **DOCUMENTING IMPOVERISHED SLUMS**
   - **IMPOVERISHED – very poor**

In his book *How the Other Half Lives,* the writer and photographer Jacob Riis documented the terrible conditions endured by IMPOVERISHED immigrants living on New York City's Lower East Side in the late nineteenth century. At that time, a single square mile of the Lower East Side contained 334,000 people, making it one of the most densely populated places in the world. Riis's photographs exposed the IMPOVERISHED slums where large families were often forced to live in one-room apartments.

84. **TR'S IRATE RESPONSE**
   - **IRATE - filled with rage; furious**

On February 16, 1898, Americans awoke to the shocking news that a mysterious explosion had sunk the *U.S.S. Maine* in Havana Harbor. Theodore Roosevelt, then the Assistant Secretary of the Navy, was IRATE. "The Maine," he angrily wrote, "was sunk by an act of dirty treachery on the part of the Spaniards." TR became even more IRATE when he contemptuously watched President McKinley's diplomatic efforts to avoid conflict with Spain. The IRATE Roosevelt exclaimed, "McKinley has no more backbone than a chocolate éclair."

85. **A CHAOTIC DAY ON THE STOCK MARKET**
   - **CHAOTIC - disorganized and confused**

As the New York Stock Exchange opened on Thursday, October 29, 1929, the brokers hoped for another profitable day of rising prices. Instead, they encountered a CHAOTIC day of record selling and losses. By 1:00 p.m., the stock ticker had fallen 92 minutes behind the transactions on the trading floor. Frightened brokers could not get a true picture of what was happening. The CHAOTIC shouting of 1,000 frantic brokers and their assistants created what one observer called a "weird roar." Now known as Black Thursday, the CHAOTIC market crash marked the beginning of the Great Depression.

86. CREDULOUS PEOPLE BELIEVE THE MARTIANS ARE COMING!
- **CREDULOUS – easily fooled**

On Sunday, October 30, 1938, about six million Americans tuned their radio dials to CBS. Shocked listeners soon heard a frantic announcer describing a terrifying creature with a V-shaped mouth, "saliva dripping from its rimless lips that seem to quiver and pulsate." The announcer then grimly informed listeners that the fearsome creatures were "the vanguard of an invading army from the planet Mars." Soon, CREDULOUS people across the country began to panic, clinging to each other for comfort. Terrified families ran blindly into the streets. A Princeton University study found that the fictional broadcast deceived about one-third of the listeners. Today we are incredulous that so many people were CREDULOUS!

87. A NATIONAL CONSENSUS
- **CONSENSUS - a general agreement**

In the fall of 1941, Hitler's armies appeared to be unstoppable as they roared across Russia. At the same time, relations between the United States and Japan were rapidly deteriorating. Despite these ominous developments, there was no CONSENSUS in the United States about what foreign policy to follow. But the Japanese attack on Pearl Harbor ended all doubts and forged an unbreakable CONSENSUS that the United States had no choice but to crush the Axis powers.

88. NORTH KOREA PRECIPITATES A WAR
- **PRECIPITATE – to cause to happen especially suddenly and unexpectedly**

On June 25, 1950, the North Korean army suddenly attacked South Korea. The attack stunned the United States and PRECIPITATED the Korean War. President Truman saw the invasion as a test of containment and an opportunity to prove that the Democrats were not "soft" on Communism.

89. ONE WORD MOBILIZES A MOVEMENT
- **MOBILIZE - to prepare a person or group for action**

On December 1, 1955, a white Montgomery City Lines bus driver ordered a Black seamstress named Rosa Parks to give up her seat to a white passenger. Although she was tired from a long day at work, Rosa was even more tired of enduring the injustices of racial segregation. Rosa therefore refused the bus driver's order by saying just one fateful word: "No!" Park's historic refusal to give up her seat MOBILIZED Montgomery's Black community and led to the successful Montgomery Bus Boycott. The boycott played a key role in MOBILIZING the Civil Rights Movement.

90. FANNIE LOU HAMER REFUSES TO BE APPEASED
- **APPEASE - to make peace by giving into demands**

Fannie Lou Hamer was a Black civil rights activist living in Mississippi during the 1960s. In 1964, an all-white and anti-civil rights delegation represented Mississippi at the Democratic National Convention. As Vice-Chair of the rival Mississippi Freedom Democratic Party (MFDP), Hamer challenged the credentials of the regular delegation on the grounds that it did not represent all citizens of her state. Democratic leaders attempted to APPEASE the MFDP by offering the delegation two non-voting seats. Led by Hamer, the MFDP rejected the "compromise" as a misguided attempt at APPEASEMENT. She reminded Democratic Party leaders, "Nobody's free until everybody's free."

CHAPTER 10

THE DSAT AND THE MIGHTY PREFIX

A prefix is a word part placed before a root in order to direct or change the root's meaning. Prefixes are short but mighty. This chapter will examine DSAT words that use the prefixes E-, EX-, RE-, and DE-. Taken together, these "Big Three" prefixes will help you remember the meanings of many DSAT vocabulary words.

E- and EX-: We are OUT of here!

91.   MEMORABLE ECCENTRICS
   - **ECCENTRIC – Literally OUT of the center and thus unconventional**

What do Doctor Emmett L. Brown in the *Back to the Future* movies and Doctor Stephen Strange in the Marvel Cinematic Universe movies have in common? Both are ECCENTRIC! Doctor Brown is the "Mad Scientist" who invented the DeLorean time machine. Doctor Strange is the brilliant but arrogant "Sorcerer Supreme" who more than lives up to his reputation as an ECCENTRIC but powerful magician whose spells affect all the superheroes and villains.

92.   EVINCE FEELINGS
   - **EVINCE – to literally put one's feelings OUT so others can see them**

In the beginning of the Official Music Video for *Dance the Night Away*, the Chief Choreographer calls Dua Lipa aside and quickly shows her new steps for the dance. No problem! Dua EVINCES complete confidence saying, "I love that!" In fact, she doesn't miss a step and needless to say, "not one hair is out of place." No doubt, some other artists would have EVINCED complete confusion and been forced to ask the choreographer to slowly review each new step.

93. DUA LIPA'S DIAMOND ELICITS ASTONISHED LOOKS
- **ELICIT – to draw OUT, usually a response**

All eyes focused on Dua Lipa as she confidently walked down the red carpet at the 2023 Met Gala. As one of the co-hosts of the star-studded event, Lipa had to deliver a glamorous look that would ELICIT astonished looks from the other celebrities. The pop star didn't disappoint! Although Lipa wore a stunning Chanel white gown trimmed with black lace, all eyes were riveted on her dazzling diamond necklace. Known as the Legendary Diamond, the Tiffany jewel weighs over 100 carats and is reportedly worth over $10 million. No wonder Dua Lipa ELICITED astonished gasps from the gala guests.

RE-: We're BACK AGAIN!

94. WILL MILEY AND LIAM RECONCILE?
- **RECONCILE – to bring two opposing people or things back together**

Miley Cyrus and Liam Hemsworth first met and fell in love as teenagers. In the following years, they had a passionate, on-and-off romance with breakups followed by tearful RECONCILIATIONS that ultimately led to marriage. However, their marriage lasted less than a year. Will Miley and Liam RECONCILE one again? Probably not. Miley's hit song "Flowers" seems to be a none-too-subtle declaration that she is enjoying her independence and that a RECONCILIATION is very unlikely.

95. ELTON JOHN REPLISHES HIS SUPPLY OF HIT SONGS
- **REPLENISH – to fill up AGAIN; resupply**

The COVID-19 pandemic forced Elton John to pause his Farewell Yellow Brick Road tour. Although his legendary career has included an incredible number of hit songs, John felt a need to REPLENISH his repertoire of songs by working with different artists. Mission accomplished! Called the Lockdown Sessions, John's new album features hit songs with a diverse group of artists that includes Dua Lipa, Charlie Puth, and Stevie Wonder.

96. WOULD MARTIN LUTHER RENOUNCE HIS WRITINGS?
- **RENOUNCE – to take BACK**

Have you ever been pressured to RENOUNCE a strongly held opinion? If so, you know what Martin Luther experienced at the Diet of Worms in 1521. Over the previous four years, Luther had written many pamphlets accusing Catholic bishops, archbishops, and even the pope of straying from Jesus' biblical teachings. Needless to say, Church leaders considered Luther a dangerous troublemaker. Emperor Charles V and other powerful officials watched intently as a leading theologian demanded that Luther RENOUNCE his writings.

97. WOULD LUTHER RECANT?
- **RECANT – to withdraw, take BACK; retract**

The moment of truth had now arrived for Martin Luther. Would he RECANT his words? Luther left no doubt about his position when he forcefully declared, "I cannot, I will not RECANT these words. For to do so is to go against conscience. Here I stand!" Luther's courageous answer helped spark the Protestant Reformation.

DE-: We're going DOWN!

98. BARBIE IS FEELING DESPONDENT
- **DESPONDENT – depressed and DOWN**

Although Barbie's trip to the Real World is brief, it leaves her with many unanswered questions. Upon returning to Barbie Land, she receives yet another jolt when she discovers the changes the Kens are in the process of making. The now deeply DESPONDENT Barbie vividly explains why she is feeling down and depressed, lamenting that she is not intelligent enough to be a brain surgeon, or fly a plane, or even just be an interesting person. This DESPONDENT Barbie is a far cry from the carefree character who once happily danced the night away.

99. DETRACTORS ARE INEVITABLE
- **DETRACTOR – a critic who puts DOWN new ideas or inventions**

Creating new inventions is never easy. DETRACTORS are always ready to find fault and criticize a new idea. For example, on January 9, 2007, Steve Jobs unveiled the iPhone when he announced to a cheering crowd at the Macworld Expo, "Today, Apple is going to reinvent the phone." But Steve Ballmer, the CEO of Microsoft, disagreed with Jobs and confidently predicted: "There is no chance of the iPhone gaining significant market share." Wrong! Today, Ballmer is remembered as a DETRACTOR who put down a historic innovation.

100. GOOMBAS CAN DEPLETE THE MARIO BROTHERS
   - **DEPLETE – to diminish by going DOWN**

Mushrooms play a prominent role in the Super Mario game series. For example, if Mario or Luigi touches a Magic Mushroom while in their small form, they turn into their super form and earn the player 1,000 points. In contrast, the brown mushrooms known as Goombas are enemies that can DEPLETE the powers of the two brothers. Needless to say, it is important for Mario and Luigi to avoid the Goombas!

CHAPTER 11
THE DSAT AND THE MIGHTY SUFFIX

A suffix is an ending placed after a word. This chapter will examine DSAT words ending in the suffix -TION, which typically serves to transform verbs into nouns. Sometimes, the relationship between the two words is obvious—but sometimes it isn't. This chapter defines 10 must-know DSAT words ending in -TION.

101. PRINCE HARRY OFFERS SHOCKING REVELATIONS
- **REVELATION – something that is REVEALED**

Prince Harry's tell-all memoir, *Spare*, was eagerly awaited all over the world for its expected behind-the-scenes REVELATIONS about the British monarchy. The book did not disappoint. Harry revealed that he only learned about Prince William's engagement from a BBC news report, and that he was once viciously assaulted by his brother during an argument over Meghan Markle's behavior. Another, more humorous REVELATION was that Prince Harry's father, King Charles, locked himself in his bedroom while engaging in an elaborate daily regimen of headstands.

102. EXCAVATING AN ANCIENT TOMB
- **EXCAVATION – the process of digging up, usually a historical site**

One of the most exciting discoveries of the early 20th century was the tomb of the ancient Egyptian pharaoh Tutankhamun, nicknamed "King Tut." The EXCAVATION, led by British archaeologist Howard Carter, unearthed hundreds of artifacts that had been miraculously preserved for more than 3,000 years. During the weeks following the EXCAVATION of the tomb, hordes of journalists and tourists from around the world descended on the Valley of Kings. In 2022, in honor of the hundredth anniversary of Carter's discovery, the Luxor Hotel in Las Vegas opened an interactive exhibit designed to immerse guests in the sights and sounds of the EXCAVATION.

103. **AN ORIENTATION TOWARD TROUBLE**
  - **ORIENTATION – preference or liking for**

At Hogwarts, Slytherins are known for their ORIENTATION toward the Dark Arts. Draco Malfoy, along with Crabbe and Goyle, bullies Harry, Ron, and Hermione from the moment they enter the school. It's hardly a surprise that Tom Riddle and most of his followers belonged to Slytherin. Even as a student, the future Lord Voldemort showed a distinct ORIENTATION toward the darkest magic. However, one Slytherin shows himself capable of great heroism: Snape redeems himself by acting as a double agent for Dumbledore, helping to defeat Voldemort. Driven by his love for Lily Potter, Snape develops a new ORIENTATION towards heroism.

104. **HAGRID'S ATTEMPTS AT DOMESTICATION FAIL**
  - **DOMESTICATION – the process of taming a wild animal or cultivating a plant**

Hagrid, the Hogwarts Keeper of the Keys, is known for his love of dangerous creatures who resist all attempts at DOMESTICATION. For example, his pet spider, Aragog, grows into an enormous monster who nearly eats Harry, Ron, and Hermione when they accidentally stumble into his lair in the Forbidden Forest. Hagrid's dragon, Norbert, shows a similar resistance to DOMESTICATION. A vicious, fire-breathing Norwegian Ridgeback, the illegally kept Norbert cannot be tamed. The terrifying creature (who is later discovered to be female and renamed Norberta) is eventually removed from Hogwarts by Charlie Weasley and taken to a dragon sanctuary in Romania.

105. **UNDER PROHIBITION, ALCOHOL CONSUMPTION CONTINUES**
  - **CONSUMPTION – the process of eating or using up; noun form of the verb "consume"**

In 1920, the Eighteenth Amendment was passed, prohibiting Americans from selling or transporting (although not consuming) alcohol. According to the National Bureau of Economic Research, alcohol CONSUMPTION declined sharply at the start of Prohibition, dropping to around 30 percent of its 1919 level. However, as the "Roaring Twenties" went on, Americans found numerous loopholes in the law, and the CONSUMPTION of alcoholic beverages increased sharply, to about 60-70% of pre-Prohibition levels. Many people even made illegal "moonshine" in their bathtubs to consume at home. By the early 1930s, "the noble experiment" was widely viewed as an utter failure, and in 1933 the law was repealed.

106. AN INSTALLATION TURNS CENTRAL PARK INTO A MAZE
- **INSTALLATION – art exhibit consisting of large objects in a public space or museum**

For just over two weeks in 2005, Central Park in New York City was lined with 7,500 gates covering 23 square miles. The massive INSTALLATION was the work of artists Christo and Jeanne-Claude, who specialized in temporary large-scale public works. Although the project was proposed in 1979, it was delayed for more than two decades because of concerns that it would damage the park. As a result, the eventual INSTALLATION was designed to avoid disrupting the natural environment: the gates ran through areas with little wildlife and were anchored with weights so that holes would not need to be made in the ground.

107. THE CULTIVATION
- **CULTIVATION – care and growing (often of plants or crops)**

In Herbology class, Hogwarts students practice caring for magical plants by growing Mandrakes: roots that resemble shriveled babies and shriek dangerously when they are removed from the soil, requiring Harry and his friends to don earmuffs while working with them. Their CULTIVATION of these plants comes in handy when Hermione is frozen by a Basilisk—a potion made from mature Mandrakes is used to restore her.

108. A DISPOSITION FOR SUCCESS
- **DISPOSITION – inherent personality or character**

As a child, *Barbie* director Greta Gerwig had an unusually intense and focused DISPOSITION. In one interview, for example, she described her fierce childhood love of ballet, explaining that "when I loved an activity, I had trouble doing it halfway. I would have gone to class for four hours a day, seven days a week, if I could have." As a director, Gerwig encourages actors to allow their own DISPOSITIONS to influence their performances. For example, Margot Robbie's own fearless DISPOSITION shapes her portrayal of Barbie, making the character's desire to travel to the Real World seem convincing.

109. **ADAPTING TO MEET AN IMPOSSIBLE CHALLENGE**
- **ADAPTATION – a change made to accommodate new circumstances**

While many novels do not translate well to the big screen, the 2012 ADAPTATION of Suzanne Collins's *The Hunger Games* was an exception: the film was a huge hit, grossing nearly $700 million at the box office. Heroine Katniss Everdeen struggles to adapt to life in the Capitol and connect with her audience as she prepares to represent District 12 in the Games. However, her stylist, Cinna, designs stunning costumes for her, and with help from him and Effie Trinket, her chaperone, her ADAPTATION to her new role is soon underway. By the time the games begin, she has transformed into a heroine who has won the heart of viewers across Panem.

110. **THE GREAT MIGRATION**
- **MIGRATION – the movement of a person or group of people from one region to another**

Beginning in the 1910s, millions of African Americans migrated from the rural South, fleeing Jim Crow laws and seeking educational and economic opportunities in the North. During the first phase of the MIGRATION, which lasted until 1940, Black Americans relocated primarily to industrialized cities such as Chicago, Pittsburgh, and New York, often filling the jobs of soldiers who had left to fight in World Wars I and II. During the second phase, which lasted until the 1970s, new employment opportunities in the West resulted in an additional wave of MIGRATION to cities such as Portland and Seattle. In total, nearly 6 million people took part in the Great MIGRATION.

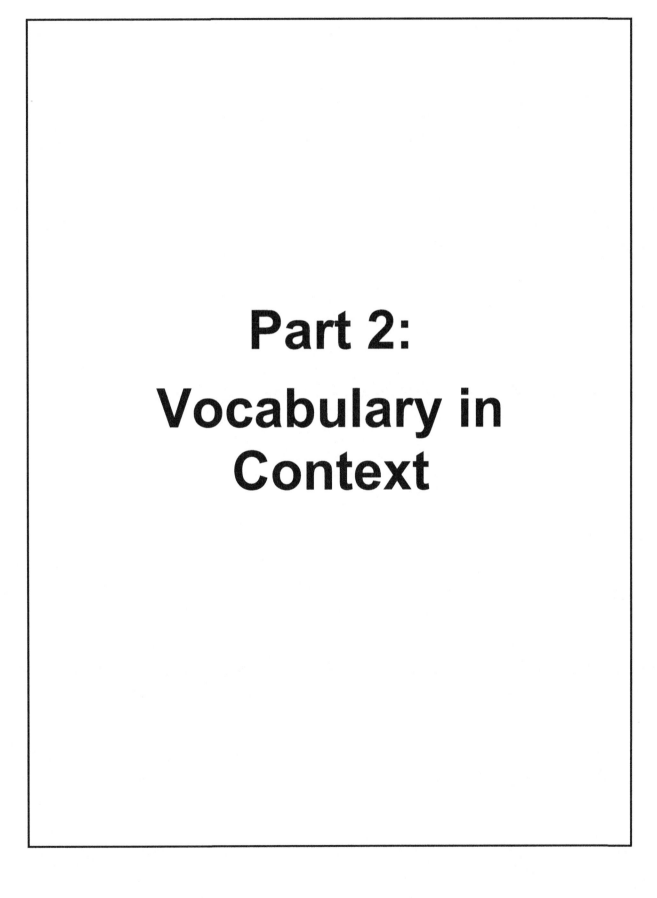

Part 2:
Vocabulary in Context

CHAPTER 12

SENTENCE COMPLETIONS: BASIC STRATEGIES

Each of your two Reading and Writing modules will begin with a set of Sentence Completions. Your test will typically contain 9 or 10 of these questions; taken together they will be responsible for just under 20 percent of your Reading and Writing score. (**Note:** Although the College Board refers to these questions as Vocabulary in Context, we refer to them as Sentence Completions because this term is simpler and distinguishes them more clearly from Meaning in Context questions, which are covered in Chapter 14.)

Each passage that accompanies Sentence Completion questions will contain one or two sentences, one of which includes a single blank space. Your job is to "complete the text with the most logical and precise word or phrase." This means that the correct answer will perfectly fit the sentence and reinforce the text's meaning. If you have to "twist" the definition of a word or interpret it in a very unusual way in order to make it fit, it's not the answer.

Sentence Completions revolve around three basic relationships between words and ideas. In a remarkable coincidence, these are *exactly the same relationships covered in the Transitions section of this book.* They are:

- Continuation
- Reversal, or Contrast
- Cause and Effect

Strategic Tip 1: Colons (and dashes) are important!

Regardless of what type of relationship a question tests, you should always pay close attention to **colons** because they serve to introduce **explanations** that will generally contain a key word or phrase. When a passage consists of only one sentence, it will often include a colon that separates it into two parts, with the second part explaining the first. Less commonly, a **single dash** may be used an alternative.

Worry About What Words Means—Not How They Sound!

Hopefully, by the time you take the DSAT, you'll be pretty familiar with the kinds of words that tend to show up on the test. However, you should still bear in mind that correct answers may sometimes involve words that you would not think to use, or that sound odd to you. In such cases, you must be careful not to get led astray by your ear. The only factor that should matter when you are choosing answers is the meaning of a word, and whether it makes sense in context of the clues in the passage. Whether a word sounds right is not relevant.

In addition, remember that **your knowledge of a word has no effect on whether it is correct!**

One very common trap that students fall into, particularly when they have eliminated two options and have difficulty deciding between the remaining choices, is to choose the word whose meaning they are more certain of—regardless of whether it truly fits. However, **if you have eliminated two options and are stuck between a word you know that does not make sense, and a word you don't know, you must be willing to pick the one you don't know**.

Synonyms

Many correct answers to Sentence Completions will be **synonyms**—words with the same meanings—for key words or phrases in the passage. Transitions, including many of the ones we'll look at in Part 3, serve as important signals that indicate the relationship between key words and phrases and the "mystery" word that belongs in the blank.

The chart below lists some common transitions that indicate you are looking for a synonym.

• Also	• Indeed
• And	• Just as
• As well as	• Likewise
• Furthermore	• Moreover
• In addition	• Not only … but also
• In fact	• Similarly

A Recognizable Pattern

The following two examples illustrate a **common pattern** in Sentence Completion questions. The passage begins with a key point or general topic, followed by a blank. The passage will then provide a key word that defines or provides a direct clue for the word in the blank. In the example on the following page, for instance, the first part of the sentence introduces the topic (Grace Hopper), and the second part provides the key word.

This pattern is especially common among the easier Sentence Completions; however, some questions may be arranged the opposite way, so that the blank appears after the key word or phrase (as is the case in Example #2).

Example #1

Mathematician Grace Hopper was ________ pioneer in computer technology: her many important contributions included helping to design UNIVAC I, the first commercial electronic computer, and developing FLOW-MATIC, the first English language data-processing compiler.

1 Mark for Review

Which choice completes the text with the most logical and precise word or phrase?

Ⓐ	a secretive
Ⓑ	a significant
Ⓒ	an unpredictable
Ⓓ	an observant

Step 1: Identify the topic or key claim in the question.

Each passage will assert a key idea or claim. In this passage, the first sentence provides the topic: *Grace Hopper was a pioneer in computer technology.*

Step 2: Identify the key word or phrase in the passage.

The information after the colon states that Grace Hopper made *many* ***important*** *contributions,* indicating that the correct answer must be a strongly positive word that is a synonym for *important.* Note that colons are important because they signal explanations.

Step 3: Make a match.

The word *important* is a synonym of "significant" in answer choice (B). You have a match! (B) is the correct answer because it directly reinforces the passage's claim that Grace Hopper was *a pioneer in computer technology.* "Secretive," "unpredictable," and "observant" are not synonyms for *important,* so they cannot be correct. In addition, both "secretive" and "unpredictable" are negative, whereas the correct option must be positive.

Example #2

Since its invention in New Orleans during the early twentieth century, jazz has been characterized by improvisation. In fact, no other genre of music relies so much on the art of composing _____.

2   🔖 Mark for Review

Which choice completes the text with the most logical and precise word or phrase?

- Ⓐ persistently
- Ⓑ frequently
- Ⓒ spontaneously
- Ⓓ pragmatically

Again, all four answers might seem plausible, so we're going to repeat our process.

Step 1: Identify the key idea or claim.

The passage follows the standard pattern of beginning with a key idea or claim. In this passage, the first sentence tells you that jazz has always *been characterized by improvisation.*

Step 2: Identify the key word or phrase in the passage.

The key word is *improvisation* — it indicates that jazz is composed without a lot of forethought or rehearsal.

Notice that to identify this information, you must **back up and read the portion of the passage before the blank**. If you focus on the second sentence, you will not have enough information to determine the answer.

Step 3: Make a match.

In this case, choice (C), "spontaneously," is the most precise match for the key word. A type of music that relies on improvisation is by definition spontaneous.

Now, there are two things to notice here.

First, in this case, we cannot really think of the answers in terms of positive and negative. All the options are relatively neutral.

Second, the answers include one challenging word, "pragmatically," which you may not know. If that is the case, you can still answer the question, as long as you <u>do</u> know the meaning of "spontaneous" and can recognize that it fits. **Remember:** you do not need to know the meaning of every single word to answer a question correctly!

Antonyms

A second question type requires you to identify **antonyms** for key words or phrases in the passage.

In such cases, however, the passage will also provide a word or phrase that directly suggests the meaning or type of word that belongs in the blank.

The transitions in the chart below indicate that the correct answer will be an antonym of a key word or phrase.

• Although/Though	• Meanwhile
• But	• Nevertheless
• In comparison / contrast	• On the other hand
• Despite/In spite of	• Unlike
• For all (= despite)	• Whereas
• However	• While

Example #3

In 2006, astronaut Sunita Williams set a record for space walks, having completed more than 29 hours outside the International Space Station. In 2007, **however**, her achievement was _____ by that of Peggy Whitson, who spent more than 32 hours walking in space.	**3** ☐ Mark for Review Which choice completes the text with the most logical and precise word or phrase? Ⓐ altered Ⓑ recorded Ⓒ eclipsed Ⓓ upheld

The transition *however* signals that the second sentence will provide a contrast to the first. Based on that information, as well as the fact that Whitson spent three additional hours in space, the word in the blank must clearly indicate that Williams's record was broken. The word "eclipsed" in (C) directly conveys this idea: to eclipse something literally means to go past it. None of the other options is consistent with this idea.

Cause and Effect

A third question type involves cause-and-effect relationships.

• As a result
• Because
• Consequently
• Hence
• In that
• Therefore
• Thus

Example #4

Published in 1928, at the height of the Harlem Renaissance, Claude McKay's *Home to Harlem* was the first novel by a Black author to reach the *New York Times* best-sellers list. Because the book had a major impact on writers in both the United States and abroad, it is considered McKay's most _____ work.

4 ☐ Mark for Review

Which choice completes the text with the most logical and precise word or phrase?

Ⓐ influential

Ⓑ controversial

Ⓒ profound

Ⓓ innovative

Although this passage contains two sentences, only the second one is relevant—the first sentence serves only to introduce the topic and provide background information (what one student termed the "blablabla details").

The transition *because* at the beginning of the second sentence signals a cause-and-effect relationship and indicates that the second half of the sentence will convey a logical result of the first half. The key phrase, which follows the transition, is *a major impact*, so the blank must be filled with a word conveying that idea. The only answer consistent with it is (A), "influential." By definition, an influential author is one who has a major impact. So even though the other answer choices make sense on their own—McKay's novel could easily have been "controversial," "profound" (deep), or "innovative" (new and inventive) only (A) fits the context of the passage.

Additional Strategic Tips

Strategic Tip 2: Pay close attention to context clues.

Many incorrect answers are included because they are words commonly associated with the topic of the passage. For example, a passage about a scientific discovery may include "innovative" as an answer choice, whereas a work about a well-known political figure may include "controversial." You cannot, however, assume that words are correct! Rather, you must pay close attention to the specific words and phrases the passage uses to define or indicate the meaning of the word in the blank.

Strategic Tip 3: Eliminate negative words about positive people.

Many passages highlight the achievements of scientists, authors, artists, and archaeologists. These noteworthy people are featured so that their achievements can be emphasized. As a result, you can generally ignore answer choices that create negative meanings. For example, in our first question, the passage focuses on an individual whose scientific achievements were considerable. As a result, you can assume that Choice (B), "an unpredictable," and Choice (C), "a secretive," are incorrect from the start.

Strategic Tip 4: Ignore all the "blablabla" details

One of the skills the DSAT tests is your ability to distinguish between relevant and irrelevant information. As a result, a great deal of information is typically packed into each passage. Although this information may on occasion be interesting, much of it is also **completely irrelevant**. You will not, for example, be asked to list two of Grace Hopper's achievements. As a result, you should ignore what Reddit posters often call the "blablabla" details.

Remember: your primary objective is to make a match between an answer choice and a key word or phrase in the passage.

Additional Guided Practice: Basic Strategies

Published in 1980, Howard Zinn's A *People's History of the United States* is considered _____ book: it was the first work of general scholarship to present major events in the United States through the eyes of everyday people.

1 ☐ Mark for Review

Which choice completes the text with the most logical and precise word or phrase?

Ⓐ	a controversial
Ⓑ	an unclassifiable
Ⓒ	an innovative
Ⓓ	a supplemental

This is a straightforward "synonym" question. The presence of a colon signals an explanation providing a key phrase—*first work*—that the correct answer must match. A work that is "innovative" is by definition the first of its kind, making (C) correct.

If you are working by process of elimination, keep in mind that the passage describes the work of an important historian, so you can assume that the correct answer will be positive. "Controversial" and "unclassifiable" are both negative, suggesting these answers are wrong.

Otherwise, be careful with (A): Although a work that presented history in a new way may have been "controversial," the clue in the sentence does not point to this word. "Unclassifiable" (unable to be categorized) does not make sense because Zinn's book is clearly identified as a work of historical non-fiction. Something that is "supplemental" acts as a supplement, or add-on. While Zinn's book may have been used as a supplement to other, more traditional works, this word is not a "logical and precise" match for the key phrase.

In comparison to its more _____ counterparts, some of which have only a few remaining speakers, the Tuvan language is spoken by nearly 250,000 people and remains relatively robust.

2 ☐ Mark for Review

Which choice completes the text with the most logical and precise word or phrase?

Ⓐ	obscure
Ⓑ	widespread
Ⓒ	intriguing
Ⓓ	complex

The transition *In comparison* at the beginning of the sentence signals that the sentence will focus on a difference between Tuvan and other languages. The fact that Tuvan is *spoken by nearly 250,000 people and remains relatively robust* (strong) indicates that the blank must be filled with a word meaning the opposite. In this context, "obscure" (extremely rare) is a direct antonym, making (A) correct. "Widespread" is a synonym, which in this case is the exact <u>opposite</u> of the required word. Neither "intriguing" (fascinating) nor "complex" is a match for the clue in the sentence.

In the mid-1980s, paleontologists began to unearth the first evidence of feathered dinosaurs. The notion of soft, colorful creatures gained such rapid popularity among researchers that it virtually _____ the conventional image of scaly reptiles within just a few years.

3 ⬚ Mark for Review

Which choice completes the text with the most logical transition?

Ⓐ galvanized

Ⓑ exploited

Ⓒ engendered

Ⓓ supplanted

The key phrase *such rapid popularity that…* indicates that the blank will describe a logical result of researchers' rapid attachment to the idea that dinosaurs had feathers. The correct word must therefore mean something like "replaced." That is the definition of "supplanted" (NOT to be confused with "supplemented"), so (D) is correct. "Galvanized" (energized) has the opposite of the required meaning, as does "engendered" (gave rise to). "Exploited" (took advantage of) makes no sense in context.

CHAPTER 13

SENTENCE COMPLETIONS: ADVANCED STRATEGIES

The initial Sentence Completions in Reading and Writing Module 1, and sometimes in Module 2, normally follow the straightforward blank-synonym or synonym-blank pattern discussed in the previous chapter. In contrast, many of the later Sentence Completions, particularly in the more challenging Module 2, are what one puzzled test-taker called "crazy hard." Or, as one student who recently sat for the DSAT lamented, "the College Board dropped a vocabulary bomb on me." The student had a valid point.

What are the characteristics of "crazy hard" Sentence Completions? First and foremost, these questions test your knowledge of difficult vocabulary words—which can appear as key words within the passage as well as the answer choices.

Second, in comparison to their easier counterparts, challenging questions are less likely to provide direct synonyms; instead, they use examples intended to guide you to the "most logical" word or phrase, requiring you to put multiple pieces of information together yourself to figure out the required definition.

Finally, while certain easier Sentence Completions may ask you to match antonyms, the most challenging questions may present negative constructions, in more complex ways, requiring you to use a negative word to convey a positive idea or vice versa. **In the hardest questions, they may also use examples or indirect explanations to illustrate definitions.**

Don't worry, though—we have your back! After studying the examples, strategies, and tips in this chapter, you will be prepared to successfully attack and answer these challenging questions.

Starting on the next page, we're going to look at some examples.

Hard Words

The good news about these questions is that they are phrased in relatively straightforward ways, with clear markers in the passage indicating synonym/antonym relationships between key words and phrases and the word in the blank. The bad news, however, is that multiple, or all, answer choices will consist of challenging vocabulary words whose meanings you must either know or be able to make logical assumptions about in order to determine the correct option.

Example #1

The brightly colored patterns woven into Kente cloth, the traditional fabric of Ghana's Asante people, are chosen **with great care. Indeed,** they are the result of _____ selection process, with each pattern deliberately chosen to symbolize a key value such as family unity or collective responsibility.

1	🏳 Mark for Review

Which choice completes the text with the most logical and precise word or phrase?

Ⓐ	a meticulous

Ⓑ	an illusory

Ⓒ	an ambiguous

Ⓓ	an irreversible

These four answer choices all present students with difficult vocabulary words. How do you select "the most logical and precise word or phrase?" Let's begin by applying the three-step process described in the previous chapter.

Step 1: Identify the topic or key claim in the question.

Here, the first sentence provides both the topic (Kente cloth patterns) and the claim (the "so what?"), namely that they are *chosen with great care*.

Step 2: Identify the key word or phrase in the passage.

The claim contains the key phrase *with great care*, which tells us that the patterns in question are chosen very deliberately. In addition, the transition *Indeed* at the start of the next sentence confirms that the correct answer must be consistent with the idea of great care.

Step 3: Make a match.

The word "meticulous" (extremely detailed and precise) in choice (A) directly supports and reinforces the claim that the selection of patterns for Kente cloth is a task involving great care. Thus, this answer is a "precise and logical" fit.

But what if you don't know what "meticulous" means?

At this point, you should use the process of elimination to improve your chances of correctly answering the question. For example, you can increase your odds by eliminating choice (C). Something that is "ambiguous" is unclear or could be interpreted in various ways (the prefix *ambi-* means "both), whereas the passage indicates that each pattern has a specific meaning. (C) can therefore be eliminated because it conveys the opposite of the required meaning.

A similar process of reasoning could enable you to eliminate Choice (B). The word "**illus**ory" describes something that is an **illus**ion, but there is absolutely nothing in the passage to suggest that the patterns give a false or misleading impression of reality.

Be careful with choice (D), however. "Irreversible" means "not reversible," but this word is not precisely consistent with the idea of doing something very carefully. The patterns may indeed be permanent, but because the passage contains no word or phrase conveying the idea of permanence, (D) cannot be correct.

If you do not know the meanings of "illusory" and "ambiguous," you should guess and move on. Remember that there is no penalty for incorrect answers, so never leave a question blank!

Example #2

Thus far, looking for the "precise word or phrase" has meant searching for a synonym or antonym. As a result, it is easy to forget that Sentence Completion questions also include the word "logical."

The following example illustrates how logical examples can guide you to a correct answer.

The famed Lighthouse of Alexandria safely guided ships into the Egyptian harbor for centuries. Widely praised as one of the Seven Wonders of the Ancient World, the _____ structure is estimated to have stood more than 300 feet high, with a light bright enough to safely guide sailors into the Egyptian harbor from many miles away.

2 ⬚ Mark for Review

Which choice completes the text with the most logical and precise word or phrase?

Ⓐ	intricate
Ⓑ	imposing
Ⓒ	impenetrable
Ⓓ	ominous

Step 1: Identify the topic or key claim in the question.

The passage clearly states that the Lighthouse of Alexandria was *widely praised as one of the Seven Wonders of the Ancient World.*

Step 2: Identify the key word or phrase in the passage.

In many cases, the passage will provide a direct synonym or antonym for the correct answer. However, this question presents a new challenge because the passage does not provide a precise word or phrase. Instead, it cites specific **examples** of why the Lighthouse of Alexandria was praised as one of the Seven Wonders of the Ancient World.

Step 3: Make a match.

The examples tell you that the Lighthouse of Alexandria was very tall and had a very bright guiding light. These physical details logically point you toward Choice (B) since "imposing" means impressive in appearance.

But what do you do if "imposing" leaves you baffled? At this point, you should use the process of elimination to improve your chances of correctly answering the question. For example, you can improve your odds by eliminating Choice (C). "Impenetrable" means impossible to enter, and the passage clearly states that the Lighthouse of Alexandria safely guided ships into the Egyptian harbor. A similar process of reasoning could enable you to eliminate "ominous" since it is a negative word that means "alarming and threatening."

Eliminating Choices (C) and (D) significantly improves your odds of correctly answering the question. To reiterate: there is no penalty for an incorrect answer, so never leave a question blank! If you do not know that "imposing" means "impressive in appearance" and "intricate" means "complex," guess and move on to the next question.

Negative Constructions

In the examples we've looked at, the primary difficulty involved the words in the answer choices. In other cases, however, the main challenge will lie in the wording of the *passage*. In such cases, the answers may involve relatively common words; however, the logic of the passage may be challenging to follow, and you will need to read very carefully to determine the required definition.

In some cases, the key portion of the passage will include some type of negation. As we saw in the previous chapter, some Sentence Completions require you to find antonyms for key words in the passage. But whereas easier passages signal this in a straightforward way, for example with transitions such as *but* and *although*, more challenging questions rely on subtler constructions. You may, for example, be asked to find a word that has *less* of a certain quality, or that occurs *rarely*.

In particular, you must be very careful with **double negatives**, in which a negation in the passage, e.g., *not*, is paired with a negative correct answer to create a **positive idea**.

Examples of double negatives:

- Not impossible = possible
- Not unimportant = important
- Not inevitable = may happen

Let's look at how this works in the context of a passage.

Example #3

Aung San Suu Kyi has spent much of her life in seclusion, yet she is **by no means** an _____ figure. An author and diplomat as well as the 1991 Nobel Peace Prize Laureate, she is recognized as one of the most important political figures of the twenty-first century.

3 🔖 Mark for Review

Which choice completes the text with the most logical and precise word or phrase?

Ⓐ ephemeral

Ⓑ impressive

Ⓒ irrelevant

Ⓓ influential

The key phrase *by no means* means "not at all," so the blank must be filled with a word describing something that Suu Kyi is NOT.

As we've seen, this is how antonym questions typically work. Here, however, there is a twist in the correct answer. Because the passage clearly indicates that the figure in question is *one of the most important political figures of the twenty-first century*, the correct answer must convey a **positive idea**. But because of the negation that precedes the blank, **the word itself must be negative**. Remember: two negative words = positive idea.

"Impressive" and "influential" are both positive, so (B) and (D) can be eliminated. These words describe what Suu Kyi <u>is</u>, whereas we are looking for something she <u>isn't</u>.

If you don't know what "ephemeral" (short-lived) means, leave it and focus on "irrelevant."

"Irrelevant" fits because it is the <u>opposite</u> of *important*: to say that Suu Kyi is *by no means irrelevant* means that she is actually very relevant. (C) is a precise fit for the sentence, making it the answer. You do not need to worry about (A) at all; whether you know the meaning of "ephemeral" is in fact irrelevant.

Additional Guided Practice: Advanced Strategies

Although historians have published numerous studies describing the Pharaoh Akhenaten's religious and artistic reforms, there has been a surprising _____ studies describing the role his wife, Queen Nefertiti, played in influencing the affairs of state. As scholars such as Jacquelyn Williamson have pointed out, however, she is often depicted as an imposing figure, one who wielded considerable power in her own right.

1 ☐ Mark for Review

Which choice completes the text with the most logical and precise word or phrase?

Ⓐ	quarrel over

Ⓑ	abundance of

Ⓒ	paucity of

Ⓓ	animosity toward

Ignore the second sentence and focus on the first because it provides all the information you need to answer this question. This sentence sets up a contrast between the *numerous studies* on Akhenaten's reforms and the _____ studies on Nefertiti. Logically, the correct word must mean the opposite of *numerous*, something like "small amount." That is the definition of "paucity," making (C) correct.

"Abundance of" is a synonym for *numerous*, so this answer does not fit. Don't get distracted by (A): even though scholars might "quarrel over" Nefertiti's role, this answer is not supported by the key phrase. "Animosity toward" does not fit because the point of the passage is that there are relatively few studies about Nefertiti, not that people intensely dislike the existing ones.

Deep in Indonesia's Cyclops mountains, researchers discovered a minuscule species of shrimp, slightly larger than grains of rice. According to entomologist Leonidas Romanos-Davranoglou, who led the expedition, these crustaceans, unlike their water-dwelling counterparts, were _____, found in trees, moss, logs, and even under rocks.

2 ☐ Mark for Review

Which choice completes the text with the most logical and precise word or phrase?

Ⓐ	anomalous

Ⓑ	ubiquitous

Ⓒ	infinitesimal

Ⓓ	invasive

This is an "example" question, so the passage illustrates rather than defines the correct word. The key information appears in the last sentence, which states that the new shrimp species is found in all sorts of different habitats on land. The correct answer must be consistent with that idea. The most precise match is (B): something that is "ubiquitous" is found everywhere.

Be very careful with the other answers. Something that is "anomalous" is out of the ordinary, and although the shrimp were clearly very unusual in that they lived on land rather than water, this definition is not logically indicated by the key information. Likewise, the fact that the shrimp were found all over the place does not mean that they were "invasive" — this word refers to a non-native species and is distinctly negative, qualities that are not indicated by the passage. Finally, although shrimp may be very small, the idea that the species in question were "infinitesimal" (extremely tiny) is not supported by the passage either.

The early European Middle Ages, which lasted from around 400 AD until 1000 AD, are often depicted as a time of ignorance and superstition in medicine. However, historians such as Meg Leja increasingly argue that far from being _____, healing practices of the time were actually governed by consistent and rational principles.

3 ☐ Mark for Review

Which choice completes the text with the most logical and precise word or phrase?

Ⓐ	erratic
Ⓑ	unorthodox
Ⓒ	palpable
Ⓓ	infallible

The key phrase *far from* sets up an opposition between the word in the blank and *consistent and rational principles*, so the correct choice must mean the opposite of "consistent and rational." Something that is "erratic" is wildly inconsistent so (A) is correct. "Unorthodox" (unconventional) and "palpable" (felt very intensely; literally "touchable") do not fit the required meaning, and "infallible" (unable to be wrong) is consistent with the key phrase rather than its opposite.

Note that although choices (B) and (D) contain the prefixes *un-* and *in-* respectively, unlike in the example on p. 68, the correct choice here does not involve a double negative.

Matching Key Words and Phrases: Synonyms and Antonyms

Select the word most directly indicated by each key word or phrase (answers p. 91).

SYNONYMS: SET #1

1 Unbiased

- Ⓐ outsized
- Ⓑ relevant
- Ⓒ subjective
- Ⓓ objective

2 Additional feature

- Ⓐ supplement
- Ⓑ lineage
- Ⓒ nuance
- Ⓓ approximation

3 Earned widespread praise

- Ⓐ catastrophic
- Ⓑ antithetical
- Ⓒ acclaimed
- Ⓓ conspicuous

4 Lacking in depth

- Ⓐ unconventional
- Ⓑ superficial
- Ⓒ tenuous
- Ⓓ prolific

5 Emerged victorious

- Ⓐ reciprocated
- Ⓑ evaded
- Ⓒ idealized
- Ⓓ prevailed

SYNONYMS: SET #2

1 Unable to make a firm decision

Ⓐ	enhanced
Ⓑ	vacillated
Ⓒ	dispersed
Ⓓ	augmented

2 Disproportionately large

Ⓐ	antithetical
Ⓑ	conspicuous
Ⓒ	idiosyncratic
Ⓓ	outsized

3 Had an enduring impact on

Ⓐ	legacy
Ⓑ	domestication
Ⓒ	paucity
Ⓓ	resurgence

4 Lasting only briefly

Ⓐ	prohibitive
Ⓑ	irate
Ⓒ	ephemeral
Ⓓ	obscure

5 Provided support for

Ⓐ	engulfed
Ⓑ	bolstered
Ⓒ	induced
Ⓓ	satiated

SYNONYMS: SET #3

1 Hatched a clever plan

Ⓐ consensus

Ⓑ analogy

Ⓒ scheme

Ⓓ pretext

2 Falsely claimed

Ⓐ spurious

Ⓑ pervasive

Ⓒ ominous

Ⓓ strenuous

3 Examined very closely

Ⓐ evaded

Ⓑ scrutinized

Ⓒ idealized

Ⓓ overshadowed

4 Wildly unpredictable

Ⓐ scrupulous

Ⓑ mercurial

Ⓒ pragmatic

Ⓓ nebulous

5 Highly particular style

Ⓐ incongruous

Ⓑ elusive

Ⓒ disparate

Ⓓ idiosyncratic

SYNONYMS: SET #4

1 Did not have a harmful effect

- Ⓐ nefarious
- Ⓑ innocuous
- Ⓒ laconic
- Ⓓ irate

2 Sought to profit from

- Ⓐ impede
- Ⓑ elicit
- Ⓒ catalyze
- Ⓓ monetize

3 Gave rise to

- Ⓐ engendered
- Ⓑ circumvented
- Ⓒ annotated
- Ⓓ confined

4 Opposing perspectives

- Ⓐ nebulous
- Ⓑ impeccable
- Ⓒ divergent
- Ⓓ latent

5 Regarded as insignificant

- Ⓐ trivial
- Ⓑ ingenious
- Ⓒ equivocal
- Ⓓ spurious

SYNONYMS: SET #5

1 Considered excessively harsh

- Ⓐ draconian
- Ⓑ illusory
- Ⓒ tenuous
- Ⓓ uncanny

2 Not their central concern

- Ⓐ peripheral
- Ⓑ innocuous
- Ⓒ hesitant
- Ⓓ chaotic

3 Precise and detailed work

- Ⓐ profound
- Ⓑ meticulous
- Ⓒ resilient
- Ⓓ unobtrusive

4 Accurately foresaw

- Ⓐ discernable
- Ⓑ explicit
- Ⓒ imminent
- Ⓓ prescient

5 Remained unclear

- Ⓐ lucrative
- Ⓑ prescient
- Ⓒ nebulous
- Ⓓ haphazard

Key Words and Phrases: Antonyms

Select the answer that is the most direct **opposite** of each key word or phrase.

ANTONYMS: SET #1

1 Gather

- Ⓐ excavate
- Ⓑ galvanize
- Ⓒ disperse
- Ⓓ coalesce

2 Made clear

- Ⓐ despondent
- Ⓑ mercurial
- Ⓒ relevant
- Ⓓ ambiguous

3 Calm and tranquil

- Ⓐ coarse
- Ⓑ impenetrable
- Ⓒ chaotic
- Ⓓ imposing

4 Conclusively demonstrated

- Ⓐ synopsis
- Ⓑ conjecture
- Ⓒ juxtaposition
- Ⓓ insight

5 Facilitated the process

- Ⓐ fabricated
- Ⓑ hindered
- Ⓒ depleted
- Ⓓ induced

ANTONYMS: SET #2

1. Initiate

- Ⓐ cease
- Ⓑ waver
- Ⓒ overshadow
- Ⓓ mitigate

2. Entirely obscured

- Ⓐ illusory
- Ⓑ discernable
- Ⓒ ephemeral
- Ⓓ laconic

3. Deeply engaged in

- Ⓐ momentous
- Ⓑ resilient
- Ⓒ subjective
- Ⓓ indifferent

4. Extroverted and talkative

- Ⓐ imminent
- Ⓑ indulgent
- Ⓒ irrevocable
- Ⓓ laconic

5. A simple process

- Ⓐ irrelevant
- Ⓑ latent
- Ⓒ intricate
- Ⓓ predatory

ANTONYMS: SET #3

1   Haphazard

- Ⓐ   unattainable
- Ⓑ   substantial
- Ⓒ   profound
- Ⓓ   meticulous

2   Ameliorate

- Ⓐ   prioritize
- Ⓑ   exacerbate
- Ⓒ   reciprocate
- Ⓓ   circumvent

3   Complex and sophisticated

- Ⓐ   rudimentary
- Ⓑ   commonplace
- Ⓒ   intricate
- Ⓓ   ambivalent

4   Fundamentally unjust

- Ⓐ   equitable
- Ⓑ   insightful
- Ⓒ   despondent
- Ⓓ   contingent

5   Disparate

- Ⓐ   amorphous
- Ⓑ   indulgent
- Ⓒ   convergent
- Ⓓ   ubiquitous

ANTONYMS: SET #4

1   Easily persuaded

- Ⓐ   repudiate
- Ⓑ   sway
- Ⓒ   adamant
- Ⓓ   imperative

2   Was not impossible to achieve

- Ⓐ   lucrative
- Ⓑ   infinitesimal
- Ⓒ   pragmatic
- Ⓓ   insurmountable

3   One-dimensional

- Ⓐ   provocative
- Ⓑ   multifaceted
- Ⓒ   resurgent
- Ⓓ   superfluous

4   Quickly altered

- Ⓐ   irrevocable
- Ⓑ   haphazard
- Ⓒ   equivocal
- Ⓓ   misconstrued

5   Utterly impractical

- Ⓐ   neutral
- Ⓑ   pragmatic
- Ⓒ   momentous
- Ⓓ   irreproachable

ANTONYMS: SET #5

1 A highly innovative approach

- Ⓐ nuance
- Ⓑ exploit
- Ⓒ paucity
- Ⓓ orthodoxy

2 Contained numerous errors

- Ⓐ impeccable
- Ⓑ dexterous
- Ⓒ ephemeral
- Ⓓ impenetrable

3 Steadfast and constant

- Ⓐ laconic
- Ⓑ irate
- Ⓒ mercurial
- Ⓓ mundane

4 A strong connection

- Ⓐ intriguing
- Ⓑ substantial
- Ⓒ tenuous
- Ⓓ exorbitant

5 Entirely avoidable

- Ⓐ erratic
- Ⓑ ineluctable
- Ⓒ antithetical
- Ⓓ aesthetic

Independent Practice: Sentence Completions (answers p. 93)

SET #1

Gunnera is known for its immense leaves, which can be up to six feet long. Although the plant is cultivated in gardens across the northern hemisphere, it is difficult to locate in the wild because its _____ habitat is located in a remote area of the Brazilian rain forest.

1 ☐ Mark for Review

Which choice completes the text with the most logical and precise word or phrase?

- Ⓐ approximate
- Ⓑ commonplace
- Ⓒ domesticated
- Ⓓ indigenous

Blinking and hiccups are both examples of _____ actions: automatic reflexes that originate in the midbrain and are not subject to conscious control.

2 ☐ Mark for Review

Which choice completes the text with the most logical and precise word or phrase?

- Ⓐ deliberate
- Ⓑ involuntary
- Ⓒ trivial
- Ⓓ superficial

The aurora borealis, or Northern Lights, are colorful and _____ displays of light that are clearly visible in the northernmost regions of the United States, Canada, and Europe between mid-August and mid-April each year.

Which choice completes the text with the most logical and precise word or phrase?

Ⓐ	conspicuous

Ⓑ	invasive

Ⓒ	ominous

Ⓓ	imperceptible

Rosalind Franklin made _____ contributions to the field of biophysics: her accomplishments, which include playing a key role decoding the molecular structures of DNA and RNA, continue to influence research in a range of scientific fields.

Which choice completes the text with the most logical and precise word or phrase?

Ⓐ	lucrative

Ⓑ	erratic

Ⓒ	enduring

Ⓓ	mundane

Although Chimamanda Ngozi Adichie was still a novice writer when she published her award-winning 2006 novel *Half of a Yellow Sun*, she was praised for her ability to create a sophisticated and _____ narrative. Rather than adhere to a single point of view, the story achieves its effectiveness in part by alternating between different characters' perspectives.

Which choice completes the text with the most logical and precise word or phrase?

Ⓐ	obscure

Ⓑ	unconventional

Ⓒ	pretentious

Ⓓ	multifaceted

SET #2

To celebrate 10 years of cross-border _____, the El Paso Museum of Art and the Ciudad Juarez Art Museum held their fifth Transborder Biennial exhibition. Overseen by El Paso Museum of Art Director Victoria Ramirez, the joint festivities included talks by artists, trips to historic sites, and a biking excursion to visit important murals.

1 ☐ Mark for Review

Which choice completes the text with the most logical and precise word or phrase?

Ⓐ	excavations
Ⓑ	collaborations
Ⓒ	debacles
Ⓓ	insights

Salamanders are the most common vertebrates in North American forests. Although these creatures are small and seemingly insignificant, they play an _____ role in the forest by helping to control destructive pests and acting as exceptional indicators of ecosystem health.

2 ☐ Mark for Review

Which choice completes the text with the most logical and precise word or phrase?

Ⓐ	inadequate
Ⓑ	inexplicable
Ⓒ	impartial
Ⓓ	outsized

Electrons are _____ subatomic entities whose activity is notoriously difficult to monitor because they can behave as both particles and waves. Pierre Agostini, Ferenc Krausz, and Anne L'Huillier were awarded the 2023 Nobel Prize in Physics for successfully using rapid pulses of light to study and track electrons' movements in ways that were previously impossible.

Which choice completes the text with the most logical and precise word or phrase?

Ⓐ elusive

Ⓑ prodigious

Ⓒ hesitant

Ⓓ nefarious

Taghaza was a remote village located in the Sahara Desert hundreds of miles north of Niami, the bustling capital of the Mali Empire. However, this peripheral location did not _____ it from playing a central role in the salt trade during the thirteenth century.

Which choice completes the text with the most logical and precise word or phrase?

Ⓐ shield

Ⓑ separate

Ⓒ preclude

Ⓓ differentiate

Scholars have long speculated about why the inhabitants of the ancient American metropolis now known as Cahokia suddenly abandoned their city. Geoarchaeologist Caitlin Rankin hypothesizes that no one single factor was responsible for the city's _____ demise; instead, she contends that a plethora of causes, including deforestation, floods, and diminishing wildlife may have been responsible for Cahokia's collapse.

Which choice completes the text with the most logical and precise word or phrase?

Ⓐ peripheral

Ⓑ abrupt

Ⓒ palpable

Ⓓ ineluctable

SET #3

Moriko Mori is one of Japan's most recognized artists. Her _____ works feature complex and detailed designs that combine symbols from traditional Japanese culture with futuristic images.

1 ☐ Mark for Review

Which choice completes the text with the most logical and precise word or phrase?

Ⓐ	haphazard
Ⓑ	intricate
Ⓒ	nefarious
Ⓓ	eccentric

Common wisdom holds that emotions inhibit logical thinking. However, recent research indicates that an awareness of one's emotions can actually _____ the ability to reason clearly.

2 ☐ Mark for Review

Which choice completes the text with the most logical and precise word or phrase?

Ⓐ	impede
Ⓑ	deny
Ⓒ	enhance
Ⓓ	approximate

The Iroquois belts called wampum served a literary as well as _____ function: the beaded designs not only chronicled Indigenous legends but they also served as a form of currency.

Which choice completes the text with the most logical and precise word or phrase?

Ⓐ	an aesthetic
Ⓑ	a superfluous
Ⓒ	a lucrative
Ⓓ	a pragmatic

In the 1980s, geophysicists discovered two continent-sized blobs deep in the Earth's mantle. Because the masses were found to have iron levels similar to those of the Moon, a team of researchers led by Qian Yuan at the California Institute of Technology _____ that they were remnants of an ancient planet that collided with Earth billions of years ago—the same giant impact that led to the Moon's creation.

Which choice completes the text with the most logical and precise word or phrase?

Ⓐ	conjectured
Ⓑ	repudiated
Ⓒ	prescribed
Ⓓ	misconstrued

When he was restored to the throne in 1660, the English monarch Charles II faced a difficult balancing act between the competing impulses of retaliation and _____. Though he was swept back to power on a wave of popular support, the country remained divided by the Civil Wars of 1642-1651, and many of his Royalist supporters wished to seek retribution against their Parliamentarian opponents.

Which choice completes the text with the most logical and precise word or phrase?

Ⓐ	exacerbation
Ⓑ	reconciliation
Ⓒ	exposure
Ⓓ	discord

SET #4

Active during the early 1900s in the small town of Ise in southwestern Nigeria, Olowe is considered one of the most important Yoruba artists of the twentieth century. His remarkable craftsmanship and _____ technical skill caught the attention of Yoruba kings, who commissioned him to sculpt elaborate doors and other objects for their palaces.

1 🔖 Mark for Review

Which choice completes the text with the most logical and precise word or phrase?

- Ⓐ impeccable
- Ⓑ commonplace
- Ⓒ acceptable
- Ⓓ unpredictable

Earthquakes are often triggered by the movement of magma within a volcano. As a result, they are often considered indicators that a major eruption is _____.

2 🔖 Mark for Review

Which choice completes the text with the most logical and precise word or phrase?

- Ⓐ destructive
- Ⓑ unlikely
- Ⓒ imminent
- Ⓓ depleted

Because kabuki theater originally revolved around short comedic plays that featured both male and female actors and emphasized everyday situations, it is sometimes compared to Italian *commedia dell arte*. However, the two theatrical forms _____ in that only kabuki included puppet sequences, a novel feature that later became known as *bunraku* and added to kabuki's appeal.

Which choice completes the text with the most logical and precise word or phrase?

Ⓐ	contrived
Ⓑ	coalesced
Ⓒ	diverged
Ⓓ	wavered

Not only are false memories common in normal life, but researchers have also found it easy to generate _____ recollections in the minds of laboratory subjects. As a result of pioneering studies by memory specialist Elizabeth Loftus, a number of jurisdictions have implemented processes to help ensure the accuracy of information obtained from individuals involved in the legal system both as witnesses and as suspects.

Which choice completes the text with the most logical and precise word or phrase?

Ⓐ	spurious
Ⓑ	amorphous
Ⓒ	neutral
Ⓓ	explicit

In a 2012 study, political scientists found that voters who are polarized on certain controversial subjects become more moderate when reading political arguments in a difficult-to-read font. Likewise, mock-trial jurors in whom researchers have deliberately _____ a bias against a defendant are less likely to act on that prejudice if they must struggle to decipher incriminating evidence.

Which choice completes the text with the most logical and precise word or phrase?

Ⓐ	excluded
Ⓑ	supplanted
Ⓒ	tallied
Ⓓ	induced

Set #5

People who commit crimes accidentally are unique among offenders because they are not initially driven by factors such as money or power. Rather, as forensic accountant Kelly Richmond Pope explains, they are presented with an unexpected opportunity that can benefit them greatly if they choose to _____ it.

Which choice completes the text with the most logical and precise word or phrase?

Ⓐ validate

Ⓑ exploit

Ⓒ waive

Ⓓ reject

According to Indigenous anthropologist Carolyn Smith, weaving is a central aspect of Karuk culture as well as a physical act that requires significant manual _____. It demands great strength as well as the ability to manipulate complex and delicate materials.

Which choice completes the text with the most logical and precise word or phrase?

Ⓐ dexterity

Ⓑ pretentiousness

Ⓒ stipulation

Ⓓ relevance

Though trained as an engineer, Barbara Braun occupied _____ array of roles while living at the Mars Desert Research Station in a remote part of Utah during an immersive simulation. Her duties ranged from piloting a fitness regimen to studying potential effects of communications delays on astronauts.

Which choice completes the text with the most logical and precise word or phrase?

Ⓐ	a rudimentary
Ⓑ	a diverse
Ⓒ	a mundane
Ⓓ	an innocuous

In Mexico, *escaramuza* comprise a group of eight women who ride horseback at the same time in a carefully crafted choreography of twelve different movements. Performed at full gallop, this _____ horse ballet requires great discipline and precision.

Which choice completes the text with the most logical and precise word or phrase?

Ⓐ	synchronized
Ⓑ	subjective
Ⓒ	tedious
Ⓓ	prodigious

A series of studies indicate that fluent speakers of tonal languages such as Mandarin and Vietnamese are far more likely to possess perfect pitch than are speakers of non-tonal languages. This correlation has led researcher Diana Deutsch to _____ that acquiring perfect pitch is, for fluent speakers of a tonal language, akin to learning a second tonal language.

Which choice completes the text with the most logical and precise word or phrase?

Ⓐ	reveal
Ⓑ	dispute
Ⓒ	surmise
Ⓓ	deny

Key Words and Phrases

Synonyms: Set #1	Synonyms: Set #4
1. D	1. B
2. A	2. D
3. C	3. A
4. B	4. C
5. D	5. A
Synonyms: Set #2	**Synonyms: Set #5**
1. B	1. A
2. D	2. A
3. A	3. B
4. C	4. D
5. B	5. C
Synonyms: Set #3	
1. C	
2. A	
3. B	
4. B	
5. D	

Antonyms: Set #1	**Antonyms: Set #4**
1. C	1. C
2. D	2. D
3. C	3. B
4. B	4. A
5. B	5. B
Antonyms: Set #2	**Antonyms: Set #5**
1. A	1. D
2. B	2. A
3. D	3. C
4. D	4. C
5. C	5. B
Antonyms: Set #3	
1. D	
2. B	
3. A	
4. A	
5. C	

Explanations: Sentence Completions, Independent Practice

Set #1

1. D

The key phrase *in the wild* signals that the blank must be filled with a word meaning something like "native." That is the definition of "Indigenous," so (D) is correct. "Approximate" and "commonplace" do not fit this definition, and "domesticated" means the opposite of the required word.

2. B

The sentence defines reflexes as actions that *are not subject to conscious control*, and the correct word must be consistent with this definition. That is the meaning of "involuntary," making (B) correct. "Trivial" (unimportant); "deliberate" (on purpose); and "superficial" (lacking depth) all do not fit.

3. A

The passage states that the Northern Lights are *colorful* and *clearly visible*, so the correct word must be used to describe something with these qualities. "Conspicuous" means "standing out in an obvious way," so (A) is the most precise fit. "Invasive" (spreading harmfully) and "ominous" (suggesting that something bad will happen) do not fit this definition, and "imperceptible (unable to be seen or perceived) means the opposite of the required word.

4. C

The key phrase *continue to influence research in a range of scientific fields* indicates that Franklin's research has had a lasting effect, so the blank must be filled with a word meaning "lasting." That is the definition of "enduring," so (C) is correct. "Lucrative" (financially rewarding); "erratic" (wildly inconsistent); and "mundane" (everyday, uninteresting) all do not fit the required definition.

5. D

The key phrase appears in the second sentence, which tells us that Adichie's novel is effective because it does not adhere to one viewpoint but achieves its effectiveness *by alternating between different characters' perspectives*. The correct word must therefore convey the idea of revealing multiple viewpoints. Only (D) is consistent with that definition: something "multifaceted" literally has many faces, or aspects. "Obscure" (known by few people) and "pretentious" (having an inflated sense of importance) do not fit this definition. Although "unconventional" is a word that is frequently used to describe important novels, this word does not match the required meaning either, and there is nothing in the passage to indicate that Adichie's novel was highly non-conformist.

Set #2

1. B

The key phrase *joint festivities* signals that the two museums are working together, so the correct word must be positive and express that idea. "Collaboration" means "working together," so (B) is correct. "Excavations" (historical digs) and "insights" do not fit this definition, and "debacles" (disasters) is negative and has the opposite of the required meaning—these are not something that people would celebrate.

2. D

The fact that salamanders help *control destructive pests* and serve as *exceptional indicators of ecosystem health* despite their small size and apparent insignificance, suggests that they play a disproportionately large role in North American forests. "Outsized" means "disproportionately large," so (D) is correct. "Inadequate" (not good enough) has the opposite meaning, and neither "inexplicable" (unexplainable) nor "impartial" (objective, unbiased) fits the required definition.

3. A

Ignore the second sentence and focus on the first because it provides all the information you need to answer the question. This sentence states that electrons are *notoriously difficult to monitor*, so the blank must be filled with a word matching that definition. "Nefarious" (cruel) is not a word that can logically be applied to a subatomic particle, and neither "prodigious" (of remarkable size or degree) nor "hesitant" fits the idea of being difficult to monitor. Only "elusive" (hard to pin down) makes sense: a particle that can take more than one form would logically be extremely hard to monitor. (A) is thus correct.

4. C

Be careful with the negative construction before the blank: you are looking for something that Taghaza's remote location did <u>not</u> do. The passage sets up a contrast between the village's remoteness and its *central role in the salt trade*, indicating that its location did not stop it from attaining importance. The blank must therefore be filled with a word meaning "stop" or "prevent." "Preclude" means "prevent," so (C) is correct. "Shield" (protect); "separate"; and "differentiate" (distinguish between) all do not fit the required meaning.

5. B

The passage contains a large amount of irrelevant information; the correct answer depends only on the key word *suddenly*—the blank must be filled with a synonym for this word. That is the definition of "abrupt," making (B) correct. "Peripheral" (not central); "palpable" (felt so intensely it can almost be touched); and "ineluctable" (inevitable, unavoidable) all do not fit.

Set #3

1. B

The key phrase is *complex and detailed*, so the correct word must fit that definition. That is the meaning of "intricate," so (B) is correct. "Haphazard" (disorganized, random), "nefarious" (wicked), and "eccentric" (peculiar, odd) all do not match.

2. C

The transition *however* signals that the passage is contrasting *common wisdom* (emotions get in the way of logical thinking) with what *research indicates*—logically, the opposite. The blank must therefore be filled with an antonym meaning something like "improve." The most precise match is "enhance," making (C) correct. "Deny" and "obscure" are both consistent with *inhibit*; "approximate" (make a rough guess) is entirely illogical in the context of the sentence.

3. D

The description in the first half of the sentence, before the colon, runs parallel to the information that follows: *literary = chronicled Indigenous legends*, and the blank = *served as a form of currency* (money). You might logically look for a word like "economic" among the answers, but unfortunately you won't find it. Don't get distracted by "lucrative" (financially rewarding); even though this is a word directly related to money, it does not describe something that served as a type of money. In reality, the only option that fits is (D). "Pragmatic" means "practical," and something that serves as money can be described as having a practical function. "Aesthetic" (related to beauty) means the opposite of the required word—this term describes something whose purpose is to be beautiful, not practical. "Superfluous" (excessive, unnecessary) is clearly not a fit for the clues in the sentence.

4. A

The passage describes a theory, or hypothesis, that scientists made regarding the origin of the massive blobs discovered in the Earth's mantle. The correct word must therefore be a synonym for "hypothesis." "Conjectured" means "hypothesized," so (A) is correct. "Repudiated" (refuted, disproved) has the opposite of the required meaning, and "prescribed" (ordered) and "misconstrued" (misunderstood) do not make sense.

5. B

The key phrase *competing impulses* indicates that the word in the blank must mean the opposite of *retaliation* and *retribution* (revenge). "Reconciliation" (making up, coming together) is the most precise antonym, making (B) correct. "Exacerbation" (making things worse) and "discord" (disagreement) both imply the opposite, and "exposure" (being exposed or revealed) does not make any sense in context.

Set #4

1. A

The blank is linked to *remarkable technical skill* by the word *and*, so the blank must be filled with an extremely positive word meaning something like "incredible" or "outstanding." "Impeccable" means "flawless," so (A) is the most precise fit. "Commonplace" (very common) and "unpredictable" do not make sense, and "acceptable" is insufficiently positive.

2. C

If earthquakes are *often triggered by* magma moving in a volcano, then logically they must indicate that a major eruption is about to occur. Something that is "imminent" is about to happen, so (C) is correct. "Destructive" is a word that is commonly associated with earthquakes, but here it does not fit the clue in the sentence. "Unlikely" has the opposite meaning of the required word, and "depleted" (used up) does not make sense.

3. C

Ignore the first sentence and focus on the second because it provides all the information you need. The key phrase *in that* (because) *only kabuki included...* signals that the two theatrical forms were different, i.e., "divergent." That makes (C) correct. "Coalesced" (came together) has the opposite of the required meaning. "Contrived" (thought up); and and "wavered" (went back and forth between two options) do not fit the clue.

4. A

The word in the blank is linked to the key phrase *false memories*, so the correct choice must mean something like "false" or "fake." That is the definition of "spurious," so (A) is correct. "Amorphous" (shapeless), "neutral" (objective) and "explicit" (clear and direct) all do not fit the required definition.

5. D

The transition *likewise* in the sentence with the blank indicates that the information that follows will express the same point presented in the previous sentence. What is the point in the first sentence? That people with polarized (extreme) views can become more moderate when given arguments that are written in a way that is difficult to literally read. Logically, then, the second sentence must convey that idea as well — it must describe people who have a bias because they have been *deliberately given* one, with the word in the blank conveying the idea of being given something. "Excluded" means the opposite, and "supplanted" (replaced) and "tallied" (counted) do not make sense. "Induced" (brought on, made to occur) fits with the idea that the researchers deliberately caused the bias, making (D) correct.

Set #5

1. B

Logically, people who commit crimes accidentally do so because they are given an unexpected opportunity that they can take advantage of, so the correct word must mean "take advantage of." That is the definition of "exploit," so (D) is correct. "Validate" (confirm the truth of) and "waive" (willingly give up a right) do not make sense. "Reject" means the opposite of the required word.

2. A

The key phrase *the ability to manipulate complex and delicate materials* indicates that the blank must be filled with a word describing this quality. "Dexterity" (great physical skill and agility) is a precise match for the required definition, making (A) correct. "Pretentiousness" (presenting oneself in an overly important manner); "stipulation" (requirement); and "relevance" do not logically fit.

3. B

Piloting a fitness regime and *studying potential effects of communications delays* are very different types of tasks, so the correct word must mean something like "very different." That is the definition of "diverse," so (B) is correct. "Rudimentary" (very basic), "mundane" (commonplace, uninteresting), and "innocuous" (harmless) all do not make sense.

4. A

The passage indicates that the women *ride horseback at the same time*, so the correct word must mean "at the same time." "Synchronized" actions are ones performed in unison, so (A) is correct. "Subjective" (based on personal opinion), "tedious" (dull and boring), and "prodigious" (extremely large quantity) all do not fit.

5. C

Logically, the correlation between knowledge of a tonal language and perfect pitch has led researchers to draw the logical conclusion that acquiring perfect pitch is like learning a new tonal language, so the blank must be filled with a word meaning something like "assume" or "conclude" or "infer." The most precise match for this meaning is "surmise," which means "draw a conclusion." (C) is thus correct. While "reveal" may make sense in the sentence independently, the context of the passage clearly describes a situation that would lead to a conclusion being drawn — not to something being revealed. "Dispute" and "deny" are both negative and are the opposite of the meaning indicated by the passage.

CHAPTER 14

MEANING IN CONTEXT: MULTI-MEANING WORDS

Let us ask you a question: When you hear the word *stirring*, what do you think of? Your mind might, for example, jump to what people generally do after putting sugar in their coffee. But what if you saw a question that looked like this?

The following text is from Henrik Ibsen's 1849 play *Hedda Gabler*.

Miss Tesman: Upon my word, I don't believe [Hedda and George] are <u>stirring</u> yet!

Berta: I told you so, Miss. Remember how late the steamboat got in last night. And then, when they got home—what a lot the young mistress had to unpack before she could get to bed.

Miss Tesman: Well well—let them have their sleep.

---

4 ◻ Mark for Review

As used in the text, what does "stirring" mean?

Ⓐ	Relaxing
Ⓑ	Arguing
Ⓒ	Conversing
Ⓓ	Awakening

Clearly, the usual definition of *stirring* does not apply here. But what does the word mean? The passage offers several clues: *the steamboat got in <u>late</u>*; the *young mistress had a lot to unpack before she could get to bed*; and Miss Tesman wants them to *have their sleep*. We can thus conclude that the people in question are extremely tired and have not yet woken up, making (D) a precise fit. None of the other options make sense.

In addition to Sentence Completions, the Digital SAT may also include vocabulary questions like this one. You will be presented with an underlined word, typically within a short work of fiction, poem, or play. The underlined word will have multiple possible meanings, or be used in an unusual way. Your task is to determine what it "most nearly means."

Good News and Bad News

First, the good news: Each Digital SAT will contain one or at most two of these distinctive questions, and some tests may not include any at all.

Even better, the underlined words are generally quite simple. For example, *marked, rough,* and *endure* have all been underlined words on released College Board practice tests. Passages accompanying multi-meaning questions contain key words and/or phrases that directly and logically point to one of the words among the answer choices. As is the case for Sentence Completions, this information may consist of synonyms, antonyms, or examples.

So, what's the bad news? The English language contains a surprising number of words whose meaning depends upon context, and some common words can have numerous alternate definitions. In addition, multi-meaning questions tend to accompany passages taken from classic works of fiction, poetry, and even theater. While the words being tested are straightforward, the language surrounding them may be significantly more complex.

That said, let's look at a more challenging question.

The following text is from Edith Wharton's 1913 novel *The Custom of the Country*. Ralph works as an attorney.

Ralph had not made a success of his business. The real-estate brokers who had taken him into partnership had done so only with the hope of profiting by his social connections; and in this respect the alliance had been a failure. It was in such directions that he most lacked <u>facility</u>, and so far he had been of use to his partners only as an office-drudge.

4 ⬚ Mark for Review

As used in the text, what does "facility" mean?

Ⓐ creativity

Ⓑ skill

Ⓒ control

Ⓓ predictability

Despite the fact that Ralph works in real estate, the usual definition of "facility" clearly does not make sense in this instance. However, the passage does contain clues as to the word's meaning in context: Ralph's alliance with his business partners is described as *a failure*, and he is only useful to them *as an office-drudge*. We can thus conclude that he *lacked* some quality that would have made him a better partner, and the correct word must convey that idea.

"Control" and "predictability" do not fit—nothing in the passage indicates that Ralph is unable to control himself, or that he behaves unpredictably. Between the two remaining options, (B), "skill," is the stronger choice. The passage gives no indication that Ralph's difficulties result from a lack of "creativity," eliminating (A). On the other hand, a person who lacked "skill" at doing what he was hired for—in this case, making social connections— would be an undesirable colleague by definition, making (B), "skill," the correct answer.

Preparing for Multiple Meaning Questions

You may be wondering whether it is possible to prepare for Meaning in Context questions by studying a list of words with different meanings. Unfortunately, the short answer is "no."

Here's why: The test writers do not begin by building a question around multiple meaning words taken from a preexisting list. Instead, they look for passages from sources containing words that fit this type of question. **Their process of selecting multi-meaning words is therefore completely unpredictable**, and for that reason, we have chosen not to include a list (although a brief one is included in *The Critical Reader: The Complete Guide to SAT Reading*).

As a result, the best way to prepare for this type of question is to practice identifying context clues and using them to logically determine the meanings of words used in non-literal ways. The practice questions beginning on the following page are designed to help you get comfortable with that process.

Guided Practice

The following text is from Henrik Ibsen's 1849 play *Hedda Gabler*.

Ramsden: How dare Mr. Tanner call on me! Say I cannot see him.

Octavius: I am sorry you are <u>turning</u> my friend from your door.

The Maid: He's not at the door. He's upstairs in the drawing room with Miss Ramsden.

As used in the text, what does "turning" mean?

Ⓐ	Isolating
Ⓑ	Rejecting
Ⓒ	Excluding
Ⓓ	Luring

A direct clue to the meaning of *turning* appears in the first sentence, when Ramsden states that he *cannot* see [Mr. Tanner]. Logically, then Ramsden is asking for Mr. Tanner to be sent away. In other words, he is "rejecting" him. (B) is thus correct.

(A) does not fit because requesting that someone not enter a house is not the same thing as "isolating" them—removing them from other people. Be careful with (C): even though Ramsden is "excluding" Mr. Tanner from his company, that is not the meaning of the specific verb in question; "rejecting" is a more precise fit. "Luring" (inducing someone to do something) is the opposite of the action described here, eliminating (D) as well.

The following text is from William Wordsworth's 1798 poem "Tintern Abbey."

Once again do I behold these steep and lofty cliffs,
That on a wild secluded scene impress
Thoughts of more <u>deep</u> seclusion; and connect
The landscape with the quiet of the sky.

As used in the text, what does "deep" most nearly mean?

Ⓐ	Mysterious
Ⓑ	Profound
Ⓒ	Submerged
Ⓓ	Bottomless

The speaker is marveling at the impressive natural surroundings (*steep and lofty cliffs*) and reflecting on the fact that they increase his desire for *seclusion* (solitude). Although the passage does not contain a direct synonym or antonym for the underlined word, there is only one logical meaning: essentially, the speaker is indicating that the dramatic scenery gives, or transmits, to him thoughts of becoming even more secluded. The blank must therefore be filled with a word conveying the idea of greater, or more intense, seclusion.

The most precise fit for this meaning is (B), "profound": a common second meaning of *deep*, it also conveys the speaker's sense of awe at nature.

Playing process of elimination, the landscape in question is described only as secluded, which is not the same thing as being mysterious. That eliminates (A). "Submerged" (underwater) and "Bottomless" are both words associated with the literal meaning of *deep*, but neither is consistent with the passage's implication of awe and intensity of feeling.

The following text is from Gwendolyn Brooks's 1953 novel *Maud Martha*.

What she wanted to dream, and dreamed, was her <u>affair</u>. It pleased her to dwell upon color and soft bready textures and light, on a complex beauty, on gemlike surfaces. What was the matter with that? Besides, who could safely swear that she would never be able to make her dream come true for herself?

3 ☐ Mark for Review

As used in the text, what does "affair" mean?

Ⓐ	Concern
Ⓑ	Adventure
Ⓒ	Incident
Ⓓ	Attachment

Although the underlined word is never explicitly defined, its meaning is suggested throughout the passage. The questions in the last two sentences indicate that Maud Martha is more interested in focusing on her dreams than worrying about what other people might think of them, or how they might criticize her for being unrealistic. In this context, Maud Martha's dream was no one else's business, i.e., it was her "concern"—note that this word does not always have a negative connotation. (A) is thus correct.

Even if you are uncertain about the other choices, you can still find the answer through process of elimination. Neither "adventure" nor "attachment" conveys the idea that Maud Martha's dreams are her business, eliminating (B) and (D). (C) can be gotten rid of as well because "incident," unlike "concern," always carries a more strongly negative connotation.

In the following pages, you can try some questions on your own.

Independent Practice

The following text is from Agatha Christie's 1922 novel *The Secret Adversary*. Prudence "Tuppence" Cowley is meeting her childhood friend Tommy.

"My dear child," interrupted Tuppence, "there is nothing I do not know about the cost of living. Here we are at Lyons', and we will each of us pay for our own. That's it!" And Tuppence led the way upstairs. The place was full, and they wandered about looking for a table, <u>catching</u> odds and ends of conversation as they did so.

1 ⊡ Mark for Review

As used in the text, what does "catching" most nearly mean?

Ⓐ	Receiving
Ⓑ	Overhearing
Ⓒ	Capturing
Ⓓ	Discovering

The following text is from Jane Austen's 1811 novel *Sense and Sensibility*. Mrs. John Dashwood and her husband have inherited Norland from Mr. Dashwood's father.

Mrs. John Dashwood now installed herself mistress of Norland; and her mother and sisters-in-law were degraded to the condition of visitors. As such, however, they were treated by her with quiet civility; and by her husband with as much kindness as he could feel towards anybody beyond himself, his wife, and their child. He really <u>pressed</u> them, with some earnestness, to consider Norland as their home; and, as no plan appeared so eligible to Mrs. Dashwood as remaining there till she could accommodate herself with a house in the neighborhood, his invitation was accepted.

2 ⊡ Mark for Review

As used in the text, what does "pressed" most nearly mean?

Ⓐ	Encouraged
Ⓑ	Forced
Ⓒ	Required
Ⓓ	Permitted

The following text is from Jessie Redmon Fauset's 1927 poem "Noblesse Oblige."

What a silly thing is pride!
Lolotte bares her heart.
Heedless that each runner <u>reads</u>
All her thoughts and all her needs.
What I hide with my soul's life
Lolotte tells with tear and cry.

3   Mark for Review

As used in the text, what does "reads" most nearly mean?

Ⓐ	Challenges
Ⓑ	Understands
Ⓒ	Perceives
Ⓓ	Analyzes

The following text is from Oscar Wilde's 1895 play *An Ideal Husband*. Lord Goring and Mabel are guests at a party.

Mabel Chiltern: You might have followed us. Pursuit would have been only polite. I don't think I like you at all this evening!

Lord Goring: I like you immensely.

Mabel Chiltern: Well, I wish you'd show it in a more <u>marked</u> way!

4   Mark for Review

As used in the text, what does "marked" most nearly mean?

Ⓐ	Emphatic
Ⓑ	Famous
Ⓒ	Suspicious
Ⓓ	Peculiar

The following text is from Gwendolyn Bennett's 1926 poem "Street Lamps in Early Spring."

Night wears a garment
All velvet soft, all violet blue …
And over her face she <u>draws</u> a veil
As shimmering fine as floating dew …
And here and there
In the black of her hair
The subtle hands of Night
Move slowly with their gem-starred light.

5   Mark for Review

As used in the text, what does "draws" most nearly mean?

Ⓐ	Creates
Ⓑ	Hides
Ⓒ	Traces
Ⓓ	Pulls

Explanations: Multi-Meaning Words, Independent Practice

1. B

The phrase *odds and ends of <u>conversation</u>* immediately following the underlined word indicates that Tuppence and Tommy are "overhearing" bits of what other people in the restaurant are saying. That makes the answer (B). None of the other answers fit this definition.

2. A

The fact that Mrs. Dashwood's husband treats his wife's mother and sisters-in-law with *quiet civility* and *as much kindness as he could feel towards anybody beyond himself, his wife, and their child* indicates that "pressed" has a distinctly positive meaning. Don't get distracted by the negative word *degraded* in the first sentence; the following section emphasizes Mr. Dashwood's kindness. "Forced" is thus far too strong and negative; "required," while less negative, is still too strong and inconsistent with *quiet civility* and <u>*some*</u> *earnestness* (seriousness, urgency). That eliminates (B) and (C). "Permitted" wrongly implies the women were not previously allowed to consider Norland their home. Only (A), "encouraged," fits as something that a kindly person who wanted others to feel at home would do.

3. C

Throughout the text, the speaker contrasts her own hiding of her *thoughts and needs* with Lolotte's ability to reveal these things (she *bares her heart, tells with tear and cry*) so that they are obvious to others. Logically, then, each person (*runner*) "perceives" her thoughts and needs, making the answer (C). Be careful with (B): perceiving is not the same as understanding—one can be aware of something without comprehending it. "Analyzes" and "challenges" are unsupported by the text, eliminating (A) and (D).

4. A

At the beginning of the text, Mabel indicates that she took offense at Lord Goring's failure to follow her, and states that she does not like him; Lord Goring responds by contradicting this interpretation and stating that he does in fact like her. In that context, Mabel's answer indicates that she would have preferred Lord Goring convey his like of her in a more obvious, i.e., "emphatic" (full of emphasis), way. That makes (A) correct. "Famous," "suspicious," and "peculiar" (odd) are all unrelated to the idea of being clear and obvious.

5. D

In the first line, the phrase *Night <u>wears</u> a garment* suggests that the description that follows will continue the idea of wearing clothing. (A) does not fit because "creates" is something that a person would do while <u>making</u> clothing, but the passage does not mention sewing, weaving, etc. Be careful with (B): a veil may hide someone's face, but the veil itself is not being hidden. "Traces" is related to the literal meaning of *draws*, but it is out of place here. Only (D) fits: logically, a person putting on clothing would "pull" a veil over their face.

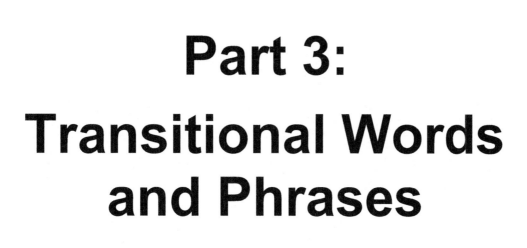

Part 3:
Transitional Words and Phrases

CHAPTER 15
TYPES OF TRANSITION WORDS

How many times have you used the words *for example, meanwhile, therefore,* and *however* in your essays for school? Most writers use these words on a regular basis.

Now, let us ask you another question: How many times have you used *in fact, subsequently, nevertheless,* and *alternatively* in your essays? You probably use these words a lot less frequently than you use *for example* and *however*.

For example, in fact, meanwhile, to conclude, therefore, hence, however, and *alternatively* are all transitional words. A transitional word signals a change or shift, and that is exactly the function these words perform in a sentence: they signal a change or shift in an author's presentation of thoughts. The absence of transitional words and phrases creates choppy, disconnected writing that is hard to follow.

The test writers are aware of the important role transitional words play in good writing. That's why each Digital SAT Reading and Writing module typically contains 2-4 questions designed to test your understanding of transitional words and phrases.

Transition questions are very easy to spot. They typically occur about 2/3 the way through a Reading and Writing module (around question #16-19), and they all ask the straightforward question, **"Which choice completes the text with the most logical transition?"** Taken together, these questions make up about 10% of the 54 Reading and Writing modules.

Answer choices to transition questions are drawn from a formidable collection of words and phrases, so you must be prepared to encounter a wide variety of potential responses. Now, let us ask you a question: is it possible for Dwayne "The Rock" Johnson to help you deliver a "people's elbow" to the Digital SAT transitional questions? At first glance, this is an absurd query. After all, Johnson is a former wrestling champion and a popular action-adventure movie star. Wouldn't a detailed glossary of terms be a better way to introduce transitional words than The Rock's "people's elbow?" However, before you dismiss Johnson as an irrelevant distraction, bear with us and read the passage on the next page.

The Tale of Dwayne "The Rock" Johnson

Dwayne "The Rock" Johnson is now one of the world's best-known and highest paid celebrities. He is a former WWE wrestling champion and stars in the hugely successful *Fast and Furious* movie franchise. IN ADDITION, *Time* maga ine has named Johnson one of the world's most influential people.

Success has not always come easily to Johnson. A talented athlete, he played on the University of Miami's 1991 national championship football team. THEN, however, disaster struck: a severe shoulder injury and a series of knee surgeries ended his college football career.

Johnson refused to give up. He worked hard and earned a spot on a Canadian football team. HOWEVER, once again an injury ended his football career and left him dejected and impoverished. "I looked in my pocket," Johnson recalls, "and I had seven bucks to my name."

Today, Johnson oversees an entertainment company appropriately named Seven Bucks Productions. He is busy preparing new movie projects, writing books, and creating material for his YouTube channel. Johnson's popularity is soaring. A charismatic entertainer, he enjoys an increasingly global reach: more than 100 million people from dozens of countries follow him on various social media platforms. ACCORDINGLY, Johnson is now shifting his attention to foreign markets because he knows the pivotal role they play in the successful career of a contemporary movie star.

This short passage contains interesting details about Johnson's career. Each paragraph features a key transitional word that directs the flow of ideas. In the first paragraph, the transitional phrase *in addition* continues the writer's line of thought by providing another example of why Johnson is one of the world's most famous and highly compensated celebrities.

The second paragraph also uses a key transitional word: did you notice how the word *then* signals a significant and abrupt change in the sequence of events in Johnson's life?

The third paragraph uses the transitional word *however* to signal a reversal in Johnson's career. It provides a contrast between Johnson's hopes for a professional football career and the disastrous impact of his injury.

Finally, the fourth paragraph uses the transitional word *accordingly* to logically connect the causal relationship between two thoughts. The paragraph begins by describing Johnson's current activities and soaring popularity. We learn that he has over 100 million followers. So how will he use his popularity? The transitional word *accordingly* captures the cause-and-effect relationship between Johnson's popularity and his goal of reaching an international audience.

Types and Importance of Transitional Relationships

The words *in addition*, *then*, *however*, and *accordingly* illustrate four basic transitional relationships tested in the Digital SAT Reading and Writing modules.

- *In addition*, *for example*, and *similarly* are part of a group of transitional words that signal a **continuation** or **support** of an idea.

- *Then*, *currently*, and *afterward* are part of a group of transitional words that signal a **sequence** of events.

- *However*, *instead*, and *nevertheless* are part of a group of words that signal a **contrast** between two thoughts.

- *Accordingly*, *therefore*, and *thus* are part of a group of transitional words that signal a **cause-and-effect** relationship between two thoughts.

The chart on p. 115 at the end of this chapter provides a list of common transitions and their purposes.

How to Answer Transition Questions

We will examine each of these four transitional relationships in much greater detail. But first, let's take a detailed look at the steps you should follow to answer transitional questions.

Consider the following example:

The highest visual contrasts perceptible to individual human neurons are ones in which the brightest white region is around 200 times lighter than the darkest black one. However, these neurons can combine their signals in the brain to allow people to perceive and appreciate much greater contrasts. _____ high-definition television images, which are consistently rated as preferable to standard television images, have a light-to-dark ratio of around 10,000:1.

1 ☐ Mark for Review

Which choice completes the text with the most logical transition?

Ⓐ However,

Ⓑ Consequently,

Ⓒ Alternatively,

Ⓓ For example,

Step 1: Carefully read the sentences before and after the blank.

Take a moment and reread them now.

Step 2: Identify the type of relationship between the relevant sentences.

Transitional words and phrases can be used to continue a thought, indicate a sequence of events, contrast opposing ideas, or establish a causal relationship between two statements.

Consider the two relevant ideas in our example back-to-back:

Thought 1: Visual neurons can combine their signals in the brain to allow people to perceive much greater light-and-dark contrasts [than 200:1].

Thought 2: High-definition television images have a light-to-dark ratio of around 10,000:1.

In the sentence before the transition, we learn that the human brain can combine signals from neurons to allow them to perceive contrasts beyond what neurons in the eye can register.

The second sentence then <u>illustrates</u> this idea by citing a type of image with an extremely high level of contrast that people clearly appreciate. The correct transition must reflect this relationship

Step 3: Narrow your choices.

Now that you know what type of relationship you're looking for, you can eliminate choices that don't make logical connections.

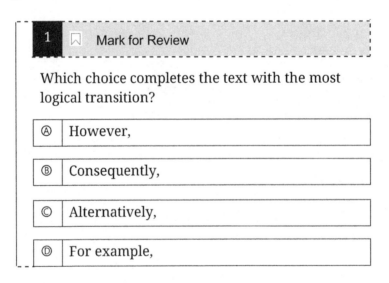

"However" and "Alternatively" both signal a contrast, so (A) and (C) can be eliminated.

Choice (B), "Consequently," can also be eliminated because it expresses a direct cause-and-effect relationship that the passage does not convey. People do not prefer high-definition television images as an <u>automatic result</u> of the fact their brains allow them to perceive contrasts beyond what their individual neurons are sensitive to.

112

Step 4: Choose the correct answer.

Choice (D), "For example," accurately continues the relationship between our two key sentences by indicating a <u>specific instance</u> in which the combined power of visual neurons can allow people to perceive images with a very high degree of contrast.

Eliminating Synonyms

Very important: if two or more answers express the same relationship, both (or all) options can be crossed out because no question can have more than one correct response.

The College Board has apparently become wise to this trick and thus tends to avoid including direct synonyms. Nevertheless, you may still be able to use this shortcut on some easier questions.

For example, consider the set of answer choices below. (We don't even need a question.)

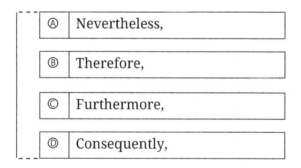

Because "Therefore" in choice (B) and "Consequently" in (D) have the same meaning, both answers can be automatically eliminated upfront, leaving you more time to decide between the two remaining options.

Thinking in Categories

When working through transition questions, it is crucial not to become overly fixated on details. Answer choices fall into broad categories (listed in the chart on p. 115), within which groups of words are used interchangeably—the test-writers are not concerned with having you make subtle distinctions.

As a result, you are best served by approaching answer choices in terms of basic function, or purpose (e.g., emphasis, contrast, sequence). **In most cases, each of the four answer choices will be drawn from a different category; provided you know the category to which each word belongs, you need only identify the general relationship between the sentence begun by the transition and the previous sentence to determine the answer.**

For example, look at this set of choices. It's similar but not identical to the previous one.

Ⓐ	Nevertheless,
Ⓑ	Therefore,
Ⓒ	Furthermore,
Ⓓ	Then,

Each answer has a different function: "Nevertheless" signals a contrast; "Therefore" indicates a result; "Furthermore" introduces a new point to support a main idea; and "Then" introduces a middle step in a sequence of events. To answer the question, you would simply need to identify the appropriate category.

Important: In most cases, Digital SAT questions testing transitions will place the transitional word or phrase at the beginning of a sentence, capitalized in the answer choices. **However, in rare cases a transition may be placed in the middle of a sentence, lowercase, between two commas.** The first comma, before the transition, will be in the passage itself, while the comma after the transition will appear in the answer choice. **It is very important to understand that the placement of the transition has no effect on the meaning. Regardless of where the transition is placed, it serves to connect the sentence in which it appears to the previous sentence(s).**

The chart on the following page lists common transitional words and phrases. Note that unlike the other two categories, the "continue" column includes transitions with a variety of purposes. We're going to take a closer look at them in the next chapter.

Continue		Cause and Effect	Contradict
Add Information	**Emphasize**	Accordingly	Alternately
Also	In fact	As a result	Alternatively
Furthermore	Indeed	As such	Although/Though
In addition		Consequently	Conversely
Moreover	**Compare**	Hence	Despite/In spite of
	Likewise	Thus	Even so
Give Example	Similarly	Therefore	Even though
For example		To this end	However
For instance	**Sequence of Events**		In any case
Specifically	Previously		In contrast
	Subsequently		Instead
Define, Clarify	Finally		Meanwhile
Effectively	While		Nevertheless
Essentially			Nonetheless
In other words			On the contrary
That is			On the other hand
			Otherwise
			Rather
			Regardless
			Still

CHAPTER 16

CONTINUATION

Continuation words and phrases signal that the sentence will give an example, add information, make a comparison, emphasize a point, or clarify an idea. They are the most frequently tested type of transition, making up just over one-third of all transition questions.

Note: For the purposes of the DSAT, the words <u>within</u> each category can be considered direct synonyms, and you will not be asked to choose between them.

Introduce a First Example

- For example
- For instance
- Specifically
- Particularly

These words/phrases signal that a writer is introducing a **first** idea or piece of evidence to support a claim made in the previous sentence(s). They may be used correctly in either the second or third/last sentence.

Introduce a New Supporting Idea

- In addition, Additionally
- Furthermore
- Moreover

These transitional words and phrases signal the introduction of information that will introduce an **additional, <u>new</u> idea** to support a previously stated claim. By definition, these options introduce a second (or third, fourth, etc.) example. Thus, they can be correct only when they appear near the end of the passage, normally in the **third (final) sentence**.

Closely examine the following two transition questions.

<table>
<tr><td>

As part of his research, biophysicist Praneeth Namburi employs the same kind of motion capture used to create animated characters in movies like *Avatar*. _____ by attaching sensors to subjects' bodies and tracking their movements with more than two dozen cameras, he can study how dancers and athletes change position in three dimensions. He also employs ultrasound sensors to see how muscles stretch in relation to bones, and accelerometers to measure how smoothly parts of the body are moving.

</td><td>

1 ⬚   Mark for Review

Which word completes the text with the most logical and precise transition?

Ⓐ	For example,

Ⓑ	Furthermore,

</td></tr>
</table>

Although both answer choices serve to support a main idea, they are not interchangeable.

As a **shortcut**, you can notice that the transition begins the second sentence. Since the first sentence must introduce the main idea, it is logical to assume that the following sentence will introduce the first example. You can thus assume that (A) is right.

You should, of course, go back and actually read the passage to double check! When you do so, you will find that the first sentence does in fact provide the big picture (Namburi uses the same tools employed in animated films), and that the second sentence illustrates it with a first example (sensors that record movement in 3-D). (A) is thus the answer.

Now, however, consider this version.

<table>
<tr><td>

As part of his research, biophysicist Praneeth Namburi employs the same kind of motion capture used to create animated characters in movies like *Avatar*. By attaching reflective sensors to subjects' bodies and tracking their movements with more than two dozen cameras, he can study how dancers and athletes change position in three-dimensions. _____ employs ultrasound sensors to see how muscles stretch in relation to bones, and accelerometers to measure how smoothly parts of the body are moving.

</td><td>

2 ⬚   Mark for Review

Which word completes the text with the most logical and precise transition?

Ⓐ	For example,

Ⓑ	Furthermore,

</td></tr>
</table>

In this case, the transition begins the third and last sentence, immediately suggesting that it is being used to introduce a second example (spoiler: it is). Because "furthermore" is the only option of the two that can introduce such an example, (B) is correct.

Introduce a Similar Idea

- Similarly
- Likewise

These words signal that the sentence will add a second (or third, etc.) piece of information that supports the same claim as the previous one and conveys a **similar** idea.

As is true for *in addition/additionally, furthermore,* and *moreover,* these words can only be used to introduce an example <u>after</u> the first example and will thus generally appear as correct answers in the last sentence. Let's look at a slightly altered version of our example.

As part of his research, biophysicist Praneeth Namburi employs the same kind of motion capture used to create animated characters in movies like *Avatar*. By attaching reflective sensors to subjects' bodies and tracking their movements with more than two dozen cameras, he can study how dancers and athletes change position in three-dimensions. _____ he employs ultrasound sensors to see how muscles are stretching, and accelerometers to measure how smoothly parts of the body are moving.

2 ☐ Mark for Review

Which word completes the text with the most logical and precise transition?

| Ⓐ | For example, |
| Ⓑ | Similarly, |

This is effectively the same question we just looked at, with the same shortcut: "Similarly" can only begin a second (third, etc.) example, and the placement of the transition at the start of the last sentence offers a clue that that is the case here. Because the sentence in question does in fact present a second example that is similar to the first, (B) is correct.

But watch out! It is certainly possible for the first example to appear in the last sentence.

As a student, biophysicist Praneeth Namburi stumbled into a dance class and developed a fascination with movement. Today, as part of his research, he employs the same kind of motion capture used to create animated characters in movies like *Avatar*. _____ by attaching reflective sensors to subjects' bodies and tracking their bodies with cameras, he can study how they change position in three dimensions.

2 ☐ Mark for Review

Which word completes the text with the most logical and precise transition?

| Ⓐ | Specifically, |
| Ⓑ | Furthermore, |

This version gives just one example, which is delayed until Sentence 3. (A) is thus correct.

Emphasize a Point

- In fact
- Indeed

These phrases literally mean "in truth" or "in reality." They emphasize an idea or claim made in the previous sentence or section. They do not, however, introduce a new idea.

- Increasingly – signals that something is occurring more and more frequently, or to an even greater extent.

Consider the following passage.

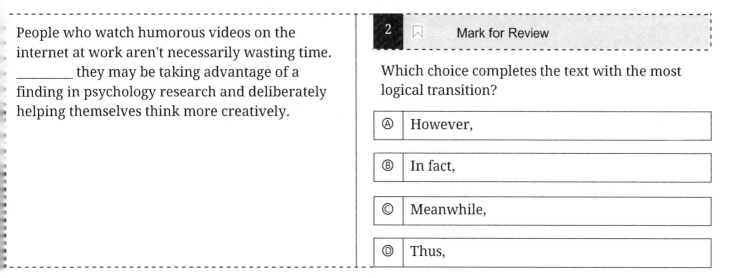

People who watch humorous videos on the internet at work aren't necessarily wasting time. _____ they may be taking advantage of a finding in psychology research and deliberately helping themselves think more creatively.

2 ☐ Mark for Review

Which choice completes the text with the most logical transition?

Ⓐ However,

Ⓑ In fact,

Ⓒ Meanwhile,

Ⓓ Thus,

The second sentence <u>emphasizes</u> that employees who watch funny videos at work are not necessarily wasting time by calling attention to research that supports this idea. "In fact" is the only option consistent with this idea, making (B) correct.

Define or Clarify

The transitions below are tested infrequently, but you should be able to define them.

- In other words – signals that the sentence will restate or paraphrase a previous claim.

- In sum – signals that the sentence will summarize the idea or claim discussed in the previous sentence(s). Because this transition is used to introduce a conclusion, it will almost certainly be a potential correct answer only when it appears at the **end of a passage**.

Identifying Continuation Words

Select the continuation word or words in each set of choices (answers p. 145).

1

- Ⓐ However,
- Ⓑ Moreover,
- Ⓒ Furthermore,
- Ⓓ Therefore,

2

- Ⓐ Nevertheless,
- Ⓑ Indeed,
- Ⓒ In contrast,
- Ⓓ Specifically,

3

- Ⓐ For example,
- Ⓑ Still,
- Ⓒ Similarly,
- Ⓓ Consequently,

4

- Ⓐ In fact,
- Ⓑ Additionally,
- Ⓒ Regardless,
- Ⓓ In other words,

5

- Ⓐ Besides,
- Ⓑ Likewise,
- Ⓒ Meanwhile,
- Ⓓ For instance,

Guided Practice: Continuation Questions

Among members of the Tsimané, a tribe living in a remote part of Bolivia, a recent study led by linguist Saima Malik-Moraleda found that those who had learned Spanish as a second language used more words to classify colors than their monolingual counterparts. _____ bilingual Tsimané used separate words to describe blue and green—a distinction not typically made in the Tsimané language. Furthermore, they repurposed terms from their own language rather than borrowing them from Spanish.

1 ▢ Mark for Review

Which choice completes the text with the most logical transition?

Ⓐ In contrast,

Ⓑ Specifically,

Ⓒ Furthermore,

Ⓓ Consequently,

The sentence before the blank indicates that Tsimané members who spoke Spanish as a second language *used more words to classify colors than their monolingual counterparts,* and the sentence begun by the transition illustrates that statement by providing a specific example of colors (*blue and green*) for which bilingual Tsimané use separate words. A transition signaling an example is thus required, making (B), "Specifically," correct.

"In contrast" does not fit because the sentence begun by the transition continues rather than contradicts the idea in the previous sentence. That eliminates (A). (C) does not work either because "Furthermore" signals the introduction of a second example. Be careful with (D): the fact that bilingual Tsimané use separate words for blue and green is not an <u>automatic</u> result of the fact that individuals in this group use more words to classify colors than monolinguals—they could just as well distinguish only between other pairs of colors. So (D) can be eliminated because it is not the most logical fit.

According to computer scientist Fernanda Viégas, large language models suchs as ChatGPT are essentially a form of "fancy autocomplete"—a more advanced version of the technology that suggests endings to search engine queries. Google autocomplete, for example, makes predictions based on millions of users' past searches. _____ AI models are trained to "guess" the next word in a series based on staggering amounts of data.

2 ▢ Mark for Review

Which choice completes the text with the most logical transition?

Ⓐ For instance,

Ⓑ However,

Ⓒ Therefore,

Ⓓ Similarly,

To answer this question, you must take the entire passage into account. The first sentence presents a claim — large language models are a type of autocomplete — that is then supported by the following two sentences.

(A) is relatively easy to eliminate because *for instance* already appears in the second sentence, indicating that it is presenting a first example. As a result, the following sentence cannot begin with this transition as well. (B) does not fit because the second and third sentences present similar ideas, and "However" is used to introduce an opposing idea. (C) is incorrect because the fact that AI models are trained to guess the next word in a series is not the result of the fact that Google autocomplete makes predictions based on large numbers of previous search queries. (D) is the most logical response because the third sentence serves to underscore that AI models work in a <u>similar</u> way to Google autocomplete (*millions of users* = *staggering amounts of data*).

By asking participants to play a video game that captured user information and tracked navigational challenges, researchers led by Pablo Fernandez-Velasco at the University of York were assessed hand preference from more than 400,000 people. They found that left-handedness had no effect on performance, suggesting that the spatial advantages of left-handedness are a myth. _____they confirmed that factors such as age and education level play no role in the relationship between hand preference and spatial ability.

3 ◫ Mark for Review

Which choice completes the text with the most logical transition?

- Ⓐ Moreover,
- Ⓑ For instance,
- Ⓒ Likewise,
- Ⓓ Thus,

As in the previous question, you must consider the full passage in order to determine the most appropriate transition. In this case, the key fact is that the first sentence does <u>not</u> present a claim; rather, it describes the general subject of a study (to assess hand preference). The second and third sentences then describe two <u>separate</u> findings from the study. "Moreover" is used to introduce a second, new idea, so (A) is correct.

The third sentence does not illustrate a previously stated claim, so "For instance" does not make sense. That eliminates (B). "Likewise" is used when two examples present the <u>same</u> idea, eliminating (C). (D) does not fit because the lack of relationship between hand preference and spatial ability is not the result of the fact that left-handedness does not confer spatial advantages.

CHAPTER 17
SEQUENCE

Taking the DSAT might be a challenging experience, but perhaps it will be an exciting one as well. When the test is over your friends, family, and teachers will all ask you, "How did it go?" Your report will no doubt be filled with sequence—order of event—words and phrases such as "I felt kind of nervous **at first**, but **then** I settled down, and **now** I feel pretty good about how it went." (Hopefully, you will also say, "And **finally**, the vocabulary book by Erica Meltzer and Larry Krieger really helped a lot!")

Sequence words play an important role in everyday writing and conversation, and the DSAT reflects their significance: just over one-fifth of all transition questions are now taken from this category. It includes a broad range of words and phrases that indicate when events occur in relation to one another, and how they rank in importance.

We have good news! These questions typically appear among the first transition questions on the standard module. Because the questions are presented in order of difficulty, this placement indicates that the College Board not only wants but expects you to answer them correctly. And in fact, there's a very good chance that you are already familiar with most of the words in this chapter.

So don't worry—if you carefully review the following list and then answer our practice questions, you'll know just what to expect when you take the test.

Let's start with the basics.

- First
- Second
- Finally

These words indicate the beginning, middle, and end of an event or process. *First* is most likely to be used close to the start of a passage; *second* in the middle; and *finally* at the end.

Writers can use a variety of terms to introduce the middle action in a sequence.

- Afterward
- Next
- Subsequently
- Then

For the purposes of the DSAT, all of these words convey the same essential meaning and are considered interchangeable. You can reasonably assume that you will not be asked to decide between them.

Because these transitions always serve to signal an action that has occurred <u>after</u> a prior action, they will normally appear as correct answers only when the sentence in question is located relatively late in the passage. Note that the step introduced by one of these transitions may conclude the passage—it will not necessarily be followed by an additional sentence.

In addition, you should be comfortable with the following terms:

- Previously – signals that an action occurred beforehand, or in the past.

- Currently* – signals that an action or event is occurring in the present, i.e., now.

- Meanwhile – signals that a separate action is occurring **at the same time** as the action/event described in the previous sentence.

  Note that *meanwhile* often doubles as a contradictor that serves as a general synonym for *however*. It implies *at the same time, however…*

*Note to non-native English speakers: If your first language is a Romance language such as Spanish or Italian, remember that *actually* is a synonym for "in fact" or "in reality"—it <u>cannot</u> describe an action that is occurring at the present time. Only *currently* is used for that purpose.

Identifying Sequence Words

Select the sequence word or words in each set of choices.

1

- Ⓐ However,
- Ⓑ Specifically,
- Ⓒ Meanwhile,
- Ⓓ Later,

2

- Ⓐ Similarly,
- Ⓑ Finally,
- Ⓒ Consequently,
- Ⓓ For instance,

3

- Ⓐ Subsequently,
- Ⓑ Moreover,
- Ⓒ Thus,
- Ⓓ Initially,

4

- Ⓐ Next,
- Ⓑ In contrast,
- Ⓒ Furthermore,
- Ⓓ Nevertheless,

5

- Ⓐ Additionally,
- Ⓑ For example,
- Ⓒ Then,
- Ⓓ Increasingly,

Guided Practice: Sequence and Order Questions

Constructing digital images from the data transmitted by the Hubble Space Telescope involves a complex sequence of steps. When the subject is especially large, a team of highly skilled technicians stitches multiple images together to form a mosaic. Additional steps are then taken to optimize the black-and-white images for tonal balance. _____ color is added to create the stunning astronomical images used in news stories and scientific research.

1 ☐ Mark for Review

Which word completes the text with the most logical and precise word or phrase?

Ⓐ	However,
Ⓑ	Therefore,
Ⓒ	Finally,
Ⓓ	Nevertheless,

The first sentence clearly indicates that the passage will describe the steps in the process used to construct digital images from the Hubble Telescope. That information, combined with the fact that the transition begins the last sentence, immediately suggests that (C) is right. Indeed, "finally" logically completes the sequence of steps and is the only option that makes sense.

"However" and "Nevertheless" are synonyms, eliminating (A) and (D). (B) is incorrect because "therefore" signals a cause-and-effect relationship that is not present in the passage.

In the mid-20th century, conservationists set out to restore the island of Española's ecosystem, which had been severely destabilized by settlers. The initial component of their plan involved the reintroduction of the giant Galápagos tortoise: in 1963, the first captivity-bred tortoises were released into the wild. _____ water-saving technologies were adopted to promote the growth of native plants.

2 ☐ Mark for Review

Which word completes the text with the most logical transition?

Ⓐ	For instance,
Ⓑ	In other words,
Ⓒ	Subsequently,
Ⓓ	However,

The key words *initial* and *first*, and the date *1963*, suggest that the transition will be a sequence word. "Subsequently" is the only such choice. It logically implies a later action, making (C) correct. (A) does not fit because water-saving technologies are not an example of tortoises. (B) does not fit because the last sentence is not summarizing or restating an idea. (D) does not fit because no contrasting information is presented.

Salinization and alkalization pose a dual threat to the health of freshwater ecosystems and the animals that rely on them. Researchers have traditionally focused on salinization, the increasing concentration of dissolved salts, in freshwater ecosystems. _____ they have paid less attention to the role of alkalization, or rising pH, in the salinization process.

Which word completes the text with the most logical transition?

Ⓐ	Specifically,

Ⓑ	Meanwhile,

Ⓒ	Finally,

Ⓓ	Regardless,

In the second sentence, the passage indicates that researchers' traditional focus has been on salinization. The third sentence then shifts the emphasis to alkalization, which the passage tells us has been ignored. "Meanwhile" indicates that the two actions occurred simultaneously while drawing attention to the contrast between them. (B) is thus correct.

Playing process of elimination, (A) does not fit because alkalization is not an example of salinization but a separate process. (C) is incorrect because the passage does not list steps in a process—rather, it describes two actions that occurred at the same time. (D) does not work either because "Regardless" means "despite this" or "in any case," which does not make logical sense here.

CHAPTER 18
REVERSAL

Have you ever asked a teacher, coach, or advisor to agree to a plan only to be told, "I'd love to let you do it, *but...*"? The big, bad BUT signals a "no." Although this word does not appear as an answer choice to transition questions for grammatical reasons, there are many other reversal words that can and do show up.

These words and phrases signal a contradiction, limitation, conflicting idea, or alternative option. They are the second most frequently tested transitional type, making up about one-fourth of all transition questions on the DSAT.

Opposing Idea

- However
- Nevertheless (occasionally Nonetheless)
- Still

These are the most commonly tested reversal words and are normally used interchangeably, with "however" appearing as an answer choice most frequently.

The writers of the Digital SAT are, however, showing an increasing preference for the word "still," which is a synonym for "nevertheless" (despite this).

In addition, the following transitions may also appear as answer choices.

- Besides – signals a point that is slightly different from the previous one
- Regardless – indicates that the previous statement, while true, can be disregarded (ignored) in favor of the information that follows.

Alternative Idea or Action

- Alternately
- Alternatively
- Instead
- Meanwhile
- Otherwise

Comparison and Contrast

- In comparison, By comparison
- In contrast, By contrast
- On the contrary

Note that the Digital SAT uses both *in comparison* and *in contrast* to introduce a difference between two things, people, or groups.

Eliminating Reversal Words

Although there are subtle distinctions between the reversal words listed here, they are all closely related and, for the purposes of the Digital SAT, act as synonyms. As a result, **the presence of two reversal words within a set of answer choices normally indicates that both can safely be eliminated**. In general, you should assume that this is the case and only reconsider if absolutely necessary.

For example, look at the following set of choices.

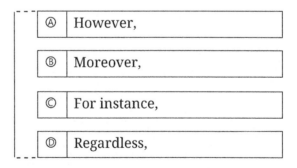

"However" and "Regardless" are both reversal words, so if you encountered this set of answer choices, you could begin by assuming that both (A) and (D) were incorrect and focus on the remaining options.

That said, it is not impossible that you will be asked to distinguish between two reversal words when only one creates a truly logical relationship. The question on the next page provides an example.

Mosasaurs were large, carnivorous aquatic lizards that lived during the late Cretaceous period, approximately 75 million years ago. The first mosasaur was discovered more than 200 years ago, and in fact, the word "mosasaur" predates the word "dinosaur." _____ many questions about these creatures remain, including how many times they became fully aquatic and whether they are more closely related to monitor lizards or to snakes.

Which choice completes the text with the most logical transition?

Ⓐ	Still,

Ⓑ	Instead,

Ⓒ	Indeed,

Ⓓ	Consequently,

If you happened to look at this set of answer choices, you might assume that because both "Still" and "Instead" are reversal words, then both (A) and (B) could be eliminated. In this case, however, you would be wrong! (This is why it is always important to actually read the passages and not just try to play games with answer choices.)

The second sentence indicates that mosasaurs have been known about for a very long time, whereas the sentence begun by the transition indicates that *many questions remain* about these creatures. That is clearly a contrasting relationship, so "Indeed" (continuation) and "Consequently"(cause-and-effect) can both be eliminated.

So, how do you choose between (A) and (B)?

"Still" (meaning "despite this") is clearly the better option: many questions about mosasaurs remain **despite** the fact that they've been studied for 200 years.

On the other hand, "Instead" is used to convey a differing decision, action, or outcome, e.g., *Researchers devoted little time to studying mosasaurs because they were focusing on other species instead.* This word is not used to signal a general contrast between two situations, as is the case here. That eliminates (B) and makes (A) correct.

Partial Reversal

Have you ever partially accepted another person's plan or ideas? What can you do? One strategy is to signal your partial agreement by admitting that a claim has some validity. The word *granted* conveys this sense of conceding or admitting that a point is true while supporting an opposing idea more fully. It is typically followed by *however*.

Online reports indicate that "granted" has begun to appear as an answer to difficult transition questions. For example, consider the question below.

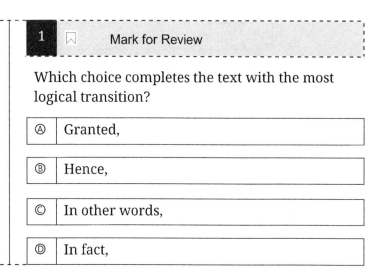

A 2017 study tested the role of humorous stimuli—a funny YouTube video—in helping workers persevere in completing tedious tasks. Conducted by a team of management professors in Australia, the study found that participants exposed to a humorous video spent more time on the persistence tasks than did participants exposed to a neutral video. _____, although the study did show a correlation between humor and persistence, the research group consisted of a very limited sample of just 74 business students.

1 ☐ Mark for Review

Which choice completes the text with the most logical transition?

Ⓐ Granted,

Ⓑ Hence,

Ⓒ In other words,

Ⓓ In fact,

Choice (A) is the most logical transition because "granted" signals that the writer is conceding (admitting) that the study did find a connection between humor and persistence.

However, the use of "granted" also allows the author to point out a reversal by noting that the study consisted of only 74 subjects.

Choice (B) is incorrect because "Hence" incorrectly signals a cause-and-effect relationship. Choice (C) is incorrect because "In other words" signals that the sentence simply restates a conclusion. Choice (D) is incorrect because "In fact" falsely emphasizes the full accuracy of the preceding claim.

Identifying Reversal Words

Select the reversal word or words in each set of choices (answers p. 145).

1

Ⓐ	Therefore,
Ⓑ	Moreover,
Ⓒ	Nevertheless,
Ⓓ	Likewise,

2

Ⓐ	Similarly,
Ⓑ	Instead,
Ⓒ	Thus,
Ⓓ	Regardless,

3

Ⓐ	Similarly,
Ⓑ	Still,
Ⓒ	Furthermore,
Ⓓ	Nonetheless,

4

Ⓐ	In contrast,
Ⓑ	Consequently,
Ⓒ	Moreover,
Ⓓ	As a result,

5

Ⓐ	Subsequently,
Ⓑ	However,
Ⓒ	Meanwhile,
Ⓓ	Indeed,

Guided Practice: Reversal Questions

Historically, Baroque architecture was treated as an exclusively European phenomenon. _____ as scholars such as Lois Parkinson Zamora increasingly emphasize, it not only coincided with but was closely linked to the rise of colonialism—particularly in Central and South America.

Which choice completes the text with the most logical transition?

Ⓐ	Therefore,

Ⓑ	For example,

Ⓒ	However,

Ⓓ	Moreover,

The passage sets up a straightforward contrast between the how Baroque architecture was historically viewed (*an exclusively European phenomenon*) and how it is increasingly viewed (*closely linked to the rise of colonialism*). A reversal word is thus required. "However" is the only option that fits in this category, making (C) correct.

Through a unique protein-to-music algorithm, scientists can map proteins onto various musical elements in order to create an auditory "blueprint" of their structures. While certain amino acid patterns can be easily translated into pitches and note lengths, they do not map well onto complex ones such as rhythm and harmony. _____ Yu Zong Chen, a professor at the National University of Singapore, suggests that focusing on musical styles could permit proteins to be converted into more sophisticated tunes.

Which choice completes the text with the most logical transition?

Ⓐ	Particularly,

Ⓑ	Nevertheless,

Ⓒ	Furthermore,

Ⓓ	Next,

Ignore the beginning of the passage and focus on the second and third sentences. The second sentence indicates that *certain amino acid patterns…do not map well* onto complex musical elements, whereas the third sentence introduces an opposing idea by indicating a way in which this challenge might be overcome (*focusing on musical styles*). A reversal word is thus required. "Nevertheless" is the only word that falls into this category, making (B) correct.

During the early nineteenth century, the Japanese artist Hokusai deliberately moved away from the tradition of making images of actors and affluent geishas who were the customary subject of *ukiyo-e* woodblock prints. _____ he pioneered a much broader style of art that focused on landscapes and the daily lives of people in Japan.

Which choice completes the text with the most logical transition?

Ⓐ	Instead,
Ⓑ	Similarly,
Ⓒ	Consequently,
Ⓓ	However,

This is a more challenging question than the previous two because it contains not one but two reversal words: "Instead" and "However." Although the presence of two words from this category usually indicates that both can be eliminated, remember that there may sometimes be subtle but important differences between two terms that result in only one being a logical fit.

In this case, the passage sets up a contrast between *the tradition of making images of actors and affluent geishas* and Hokusai's work, which emphasized landscapes and everyday life. "Similarly" and "Consequently" do not signal this relationship, eliminating (B) and (C).

So, how do you choose between (A) and (D)? Think of it this way: The first sentence already introduces an opposing idea by stating that Hokusai was moving away from Japanese artistic tradition. The second sentence describes the specific alternative action that Hokusai took, making "Instead" the appropriate choice. That eliminates (D) and makes (A) correct.

CHAPTER 19
CAUSE AND EFFECT

How many times have your teachers asked you to describe the causes and effects of a historical event, scientific phenomenon, or literary plot? Probably a lot! Causation plays an important role in school and on the DSAT.

Given their importance, cause-and-effect words and phrases currently account for about 18 percent of all transition questions. Note that all the words in this category are on the "effect" side of "cause-and-effect" — that is, they indicate **results, conclusions**, and **consequences**. ("Cause" words may be tested in terms of grammar elsewhere in the Writing portion of a module). As a result, they are more likely to appear as correct answers when the sentence in question appears towards the **end of a passage.**

The words and phrases below have appeared as answers to released College Board questions.

- Accordingly
- As a result
- Consequently
- For this reason
- Hence
- Therefore
- Thus

On the DSAT, all of these words are treated as interchangeable; you will not be asked to choose between them.

In addition, you should know:

- Predictably – indicates the presence of an easily foreseen consequence. This word appears less frequently than options such as "therefore" and "thus."

Let's look at an example.

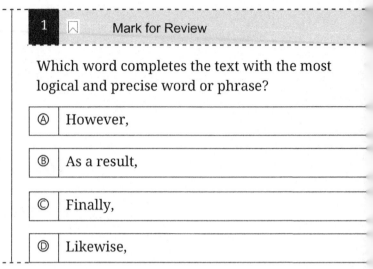

By employing wearable imaging technologies, neuroscientists were able to evaluate the brain activity of six actors as they rehearsed scenes from Shakespeare's *A Midsummer Night's Dream*. They found that when the actors heard their own name during rehearsals and performances, there was a decreased response in the left anterior prefrontal cortex—a brain region associated with self-awareness. ________ the researchers concluded that when actors inhabit a character, they may actually suppress their everyday selves at a neural level.

1 Mark for Review

Which word completes the text with the most logical and precise word or phrase?

Ⓐ However,

Ⓑ As a result,

Ⓒ Finally,

Ⓓ Likewise,

Don't assume that the answer must be "finally" simply because the transition is used to begin the final sentence!

In reality, this sentence conveys a result of the neuroscientists' experiment, as indicated by the word *concluded*. A cause-and-effect word or phrase is thus required, making (B), "As a result," the only possible answer.

(A) is incorrect because the last sentence does not introduce an opposing idea.

(C) does not fit because the passage does not describe a sequence.

(D) does not work because the last sentence does not present a second example that is similar to a previous example.

Subsequently vs. Consequently

Because these two words are long and look very similar, they are a very common source of confusion for students. To avoid losing points unnecessarily, make sure that you are clear on the difference between them.

To reiterate:

- Subsequently = Next

- Consequently = Therefore

Now, consider the following question.

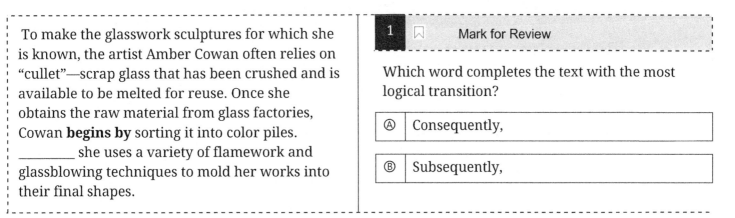

The phrase *begins by* in the second sentence is a big clue that the passage is describing the first step in a sequence. Given that information, the following sentence will logically describe the next, i.e., "subsequent," step. That is in fact the case: the sentence begun by the transition explains what happens after Cowan sorts the glass into piles. (B) is thus correct.

On the other hand, consider the example below.

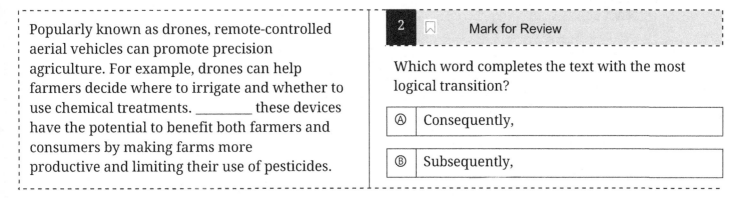

Here, the sentence begun by the transition explains a result, i.e., the "consequence," of farmers' drone use (it makes farms productive and limits pesticides). (A) is thus correct.

Identifying Cause-and-Effect Words

Select the cause-and-effect word or words in each set of choices (answers p. 145).

1

- Ⓐ Nonetheless,
- Ⓑ Hence,
- Ⓒ Meanwhile,
- Ⓓ Otherwise,

2

- Ⓐ In sum,
- Ⓑ On the other hand,
- Ⓒ Moreover,
- Ⓓ Thus,

3

- Ⓐ Consequently,
- Ⓑ Furthermore,
- Ⓒ As a result,
- Ⓓ Instead,

4

- Ⓐ Additionally,
- Ⓑ Subsequently,
- Ⓒ Accordingly,
- Ⓓ For this reason,

5

- Ⓐ Meanwhile,
- Ⓑ Nevertheless,
- Ⓒ In other words,
- Ⓓ Therefore,

Guided Practice: Cause and Effect

The presence of long lines at polling sites is a serious problem faced by voters in the United States. On Election Day in 2012, for example, an estimated 750,000 voters left their polling locations before they had the opportunity to vote. _____ eliminating bottlenecks to speed up the voting process could result in thousands of additional ballot submissions and increase people's confidence in the electoral process.

1 ⬚ Mark for Review

Which word completes the text with the most logical and precise transition?

Ⓐ	Meanwhile,
Ⓑ	Thus,
Ⓒ	Moreover,
Ⓓ	Next,

The last sentence—the sentence begun by the transition—describes the logical result of *eliminating bottlenecks to speed up the voting process*. If hundreds of thousands of people are estimated to have left polling sites because of long lines, then removing those lines would allow all of those extra people to vote. A cause-and-effect word is required to convey this relationship, making (B) the only possible answer.

"Meanwhile" and "Next" are both sequence words, which do not make sense in this context, eliminating (A) and (D). (C) does not fit either because "Moreover" is used to introduce an additional idea or example to support a point, not to convey a result.

In 2022, an international team of scientists recorded an immense seismic event on Mars. Although the researchers initially speculated that the quake was due to a meteorite impact, they were unable to locate a fresh crater. _____ they concluded that the event must have been caused by the release of enormous tectonic forces within the planet's interior.

2 ⬚ Mark for Review

Which word completes the text with the most logical and precise transition?

Ⓐ	Nevertheless,
Ⓑ	In contrast,
Ⓒ	Hence,
Ⓓ	Specifically,

The sentence begun by the transition describes a <u>conclusion</u> that scientists drew when they were unable to find evidence of a meteorite impact, indicating a cause-and-effect relationship. "Hence" is the only transition in this category, making (C) the answer.

"Nevertheless" and "In contrast" both signal a reversal, eliminating (A) and (B). (D) can be eliminated as well because the last sentence does not provide an example.

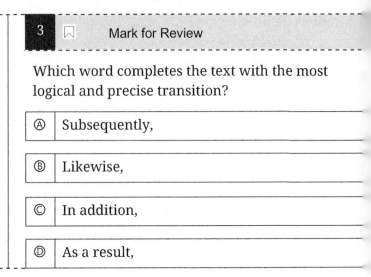

The methods currently used by food suppliers to determine fruits' and vegetables' ripeness are either notoriously unreliable or impossible to implement on a large scale. Now, however, a tool relying on high-frequency wireless technology gives produce suppliers a way to quickly identify ripe fruit as well as spot edible fruit in spoiled bunches. _____ they are able to dramatically reduce waste.

3 🔖 Mark for Review

Which word completes the text with the most logical and precise transition?

Ⓐ Subsequently,

Ⓑ Likewise,

Ⓒ In addition,

Ⓓ As a result,

The sentence begun by the transition describes a <u>result</u> of produce suppliers' newfound ability to identify fruit that is ready for sale. A cause-and-effect word or phrase is thus required. "As a result" is the only option in this category, so (D) is correct.

"Subsequently" (afterward, later) is used to indicate a sequence of events, eliminating (A). "Likewise" does not fit because the last sentence does not present an example that is similar to the previous example, eliminating (B). "In addition" does not quite fit either because the passage is indicating a direct consequence, not just adding a new, related point. (C) can thus be eliminated as well.

Independent Practice: All Transitions

String theory is a broad theoretical framework that can be used to investigate many questions about nature's most fundamental constituents and forces. _____ it is now being applied to problems such as early universe cosmology and black hole physics.

Which choice completes the text with the most logical transition?

Ⓐ For example,

Ⓑ Nevertheless,

Ⓒ Moreover,

Ⓓ However,

The skyscrapers that began to dominate the New York skyline in the 1920s not only brought prestige and publicity, but they also resolved a practical problem. As land prices increased, developers had no choice but to build upward, raising their structures as high as technology, natural light, and zoning regulations would allow. _____ local officials attempted to ensure that city residents would have access to green space, acquiring more than 2,000 acres of parkland over the course of the decade.

Which choice completes the text with the most logical transition?

Ⓐ Indeed,

Ⓑ Still,

Ⓒ For example,

Ⓓ Finally,

Common throughout Polynesia, rahuis are temporary limits on the collection of a particular resource—for example, a fish or plant— in specific areas of land or water. Eventually, when the resource has had time to recover, the rahui is ended. The word "rahui" itself has many meanings: It can, for example, refer to a management system, a practice or belief. _____ it can refer to a law or a lens through which related actions are assessed.

3 ⌷ Mark for Review

Which choice completes the text with the most logical transition?

Ⓐ Alternately,

Ⓑ Consequently,

Ⓒ In fact,

Ⓓ Similarly,

In their 2017 study of bees' cognitive abilities, behavioral ecologists Olli Loukola and Clint Perry challenged the prevailing view that bees are tiny, unthinking machines that collect pollen and nectar to make honey. The researchers argued that instead of being shaped by genetically pre-programmed behavior, bumblebees and honeybees can count and navigate complex environments. _____ they asserted that bees even display behaviors that appear to be driven by emotions.

4 ⌷ Mark for Review

Which choice completes the text with the most logical transition?

Ⓐ Moreover,

Ⓑ For instance,

Ⓒ Therefore,

Ⓓ On the other hand,

In an experiment conducted at Imperial College, London, computer scientists first programmed a device to produce loops of random sounds. Then, they asked a group of musical consumers to complete a survey indicating which ones they preferred. _____ they analyzed the listeners' opinions, finding that the most popular choices were filled with many of the sophisticated chords and rhythms used in modern songs.

5 ⌷ Mark for Review

Which choice completes the text with the most logical transition?

Ⓐ Indeed,

Ⓑ Similarly,

Ⓒ Finally,

Ⓓ For example,

Psychologist Suzanne Bell has been attempting to determine how NASA can create the most effective team for a long-term mission to Mars. One of her discoveries is that people with more outgoing personalities may not be particularly well suited to such a mission. _____ they might have a hard time adjusting to environments in which there is little opportunity for new activities or social interaction.

6   Mark for Review

Which choice completes the text with the most logical transition?

Ⓐ | Next,

Ⓑ | Specifically,

Ⓒ | Therefore,

Ⓓ | Still,

A recent study suggests that people's self-reported media habits may not be an accurate reflection of the sources from which they receive their information. For instance, researchers observed substantial variation in the actual news consumption habits of participants who indicated identical media preferences. _____ people who expressed different media preferences in the survey often visited similar online news outlets.

7   Mark for Review

Which choice completes the text with the most logical transition?

Ⓐ | For example,

Ⓑ | Thus,

Ⓒ | Nevertheless,

Ⓓ | Likewise,

For more than a thousand years, kalo—a starchy root vegetable also known as taro—was a staple crop in Hawai'i, covering an estimated 35,000 acres at its peak. Kalo production steadily declined during the nineteenth and twentieth centuries. It has, _____ experienced a resurgence in popularity thanks to the efforts of Native Hawaiians such as Hōkūao Pellegrino, who in 2004 received a grant from Onipa'a Nā Hui Kalo, a statewide organization of kalo farmers, and now grows 45 varieties of taro on his family's Maui land, Noho'ana Farm.

8   Mark for Review

Which choice completes the text with the most logical transition?

Ⓐ | for example,

Ⓑ | moreover,

Ⓒ | however,

Ⓓ | meanwhile,

In recent years, some scientists have observed that the water in their experiments, held in a sponge-like material known as a hydrogel, was evaporating at a far higher rate than could be explained by the amount of heat to which it was exposed. After carrying out a series of new experiments and simulations, researchers reached a startling conclusion: Under certain circumstances, light alone can directly cause water to evaporate. _____ it can do so in a very efficient way.

Which choice completes the text with the most logical transition?

Ⓐ	In fact,
Ⓑ	Rather,
Ⓒ	Meanwhile,
Ⓓ	Consequently,

During the International Year of Astronomy in 2009, a team of Australian astrophysicists who were working toward building the largest telescope on Earth collaborated with Indigenous artists living in the region where the telescope would be built. The two groups explored native traditions, including perspectives on the night sky, as well as the modern understanding of the universe. _____ the artists produced over 100 original artworks for an exhibition called "Ilgarijiri — Things belonging to the Sky"

Which choice completes the text with the most logical transition?

Ⓐ	However,
Ⓑ	Subsequently,
Ⓒ	Indeed,
Ⓓ	For example,

Answers: Identifying Transitions, Independent Practice

Identifying Continuation Words	Identifying Cause-and-Effect Words
1. B, C	1. B
2. B, D	2. D
3. A, C	3. A, C
4. A, B	4. C
5. B, D	5. D
Identifying Sequence Words	
1. D	
2. B	
3. A, D	
4. A	
5. C	
Identifying Reversal Words	
1. C	
2. B	
3. B, D	
4. A	
5. B, C	

Explanations: Transitions, Independent Practice

1. A

The reference to *problems such as early universe cosmology and black hole physics* indicates that the sentence begun by the transition is presenting an example of how string theory is used; the transition must convey that purpose. "For example" is the only option with that function, so (A) is correct. Note that "Nevertheless" and "However" are synonyms, so (A) and (D) can both be eliminated automatically. "Moreover" does not fit either because this transition can only introduce an example <u>after</u> the first example. That eliminates (C) as well.

2. B

The first two sentences focus on the construction of skyscrapers in New York City, whereas the last sentence — the sentence begun by the transition — introduces a contrasting idea, namely that city officials attempted to preserve access to green space as well. A reversal word is thus required. "Still" is the only option in this category, making (B) correct.

3. A

The last sentence — the sentence begun by the transition — describes a definition of "rahui" that is different from the definition provided in the previous sentence. As a result, a reversal word is required. "Alternately" is the sole option in this category, making (A) the only possible answer. "Consequently" indicates cause and effect, and "In fact" and "Similarly" both signal continuation, eliminating the other answers.

4. A

To answer this question, you must consider the entire passage. The first sentence presents a claim (Loukola and Perry <u>challenged</u> the idea that bees are simple, honey-making machines), and each sentence that follows presents a piece of support for that claim. (D) can be eliminated right away because the third sentence does not reverse the idea in the second. (C) can be eliminated fairly easily as well because the fact that bees exhibit what appears to be emotion-driven behavior is not a <u>result</u> of the fact that they can count and navigate complex environments. To choose between (A) and (B), consider that the last sentence presents a <u>second</u> example, whereas "For instance" can only be used to introduce a first example. Alternately, you can recognize that being driven by emotions is not an example of being able to count and navigate complex environments. Because the last sentence presents a separate, new example to support the main idea, "Moreover" is the only logical fit. (A) is thus correct.

5. C

If you read the entire passage, the answer to this question is straightforward: The key words *first* in the first sentence and *Then* in the second clearly indicate that the passage is describing steps in a sequence. The sentence begun by the transition clearly describes the last step in the experiments because it describes the researchers' finding. Given this context, "Finally" is the only logical answer, making (C) correct. You do not need to consider the other options.

6. B

The last sentence—the sentence begun by the transition—provides an example of why more outgoing individuals may have difficulty adjusting to a long space mission. "Specifically" is the only option that serves to introduce a (first) example, so (B) is correct. (A) is incorrect because "Next" is a sequence word, but the passage does not describe a process or series of events. (C) does not fit because "therefore" introduces a logical consequence, but the fact that outgoing people may struggle with limited opportunity for new activities or socializing is not a <u>result</u> of the fact that they may not be well suited to long space missions—rather, it is a cause. "Still" does not fit because it is a reversal word, eliminating (D).

7. D

To answer this question, you must consider the entire passage. The first sentence presents a claim (self-reported media habits may not reflect the news sources that people actually use), and the following two sentences support it through specific examples. The presence of *for instance* in the second sentence indicates that an equivalent phrase ("For example) cannot begin the next sentence, eliminating (A). (C) can be eliminated as well because the last two sentences do not express opposing ideas—both serve to support the same point. (B) does not fit either because the last sentence does not describe a result of the previous sentence. (D) is correct because "Likewise" indicates that the second example serves to illustrate the same point as the first, namely that there is a gap between people's perception of their media preferences and their actual behavior.

8. C

Don't be intimidated by the length of the last sentence. In reality, this question is much simpler than it seems. The only relevant information appears immediately before and after the transition. The previous sentence indicates that kalo production declined in the ninteenth and twentieth centuries, whereas the sentence begun by the transition indicates that it has *experienced a resurgence in popularity*. Those are opposing ideas, so a reversal word is required, making (C) the only possible answer.

9. A

The last sentence—the sentence begun by the transition—continues the idea introduced in the previous sentence, namely that light by itself can cause water to evaporate. "Rather" and "Meanwhile" are reversal words, so (B) and (C) can be eliminated. "Consequently" signals an effect, but the fact that light can cause water to evaporate efficiently is not a result of the fact that it can cause evaporation—that does not make any sense. "In fact" fits because the last sentence continues and emphasizes the statement in the previous sentence. (A) is thus correct.

10. B

Logically, the artists must have produced the hundred-plus artworks after they spent time collaborating with the physicists. A sequence word is thus required. "Subsequently" is the only option in this category, making (B) the only possible answer.

ABOUT THE AUTHORS

Larry Krieger was born and raised in western North Carolina. He earned his Bachelor of Arts and Master of Arts in Teaching from the University of North Carolina at Chapel Hill, and his Masters of Arts degree in Sociology from Wake Forest University. Larry has taught urban, rural, and suburban high school students in public high schools in North Carolina and New Jersey. His popular AP® courses and after-school SAT courses helped his students achieve exemplary scores on both tests. For example, Larry led Montgomery High School to a #1 SAT ranking in the state of New Jersey. The College Board has also recognized Larry as one of America's top AP teachers.

Larry's success has extended beyond the classroom. He is the author of widely known prep books for AP US History and SAT Vocabulary and Critical Reading. He conducts AP U.S. History and SAT workshops for students throughout the United States.

Erica Meltzer earned her B.A. from Wellesley College and spent more than a decade tutoring privately in Boston and New York City, as well as nationally and internationally via Skype. Her experience working with students from a wide range of educational backgrounds and virtually every score level, from the third percentile to the 99th, gave her unique insight into the types of stumbling blocks students often encounter when preparing for standardized reading and writing tests.

She was inspired to begin writing her own test-prep materials in 2007, after visiting a local bookstore in search of additional practice questions for an SAT Writing student. Unable to find material that replicated the contents of the exam with sufficient accuracy, she decided to write her own. What started as a handful of exercises jotted down on a piece of paper became the basis for her first book, the original *Ultimate Guide to SAT Grammar*, published in 2011. Since that time, she has authored guides for SAT reading and vocabulary, as well as verbal guides for the ACT®, GRE®, and GMAT®. Her books have sold more than 100,000 copies and are used around the world. She lives in New York City, and you can visit her online at www.thecriticalreader.com.

Printed in Great Britain
by Amazon

44693699R00084